STUDENT UNIT GUIDE

NEW EDITION

AQA A2 Government & Politics Unit 4A Updated
The Government of the USA

Colleen Harris
Updated by Simon Lemieux

Series Editor: Eric Magee

You c

If you requ

PHILIP ALLAN FOR
HODDER
EDUCATION
AN HACHETTE UK COMPANY

Philip Allan, an imprint of Hodder Education, an Hachette UK company, Market Place, Deddington, Oxfordshire OX15 OSE

Orders
Bookpoint Ltd, 130 Milton Park, Abingdon, Oxfordshire OX14 4SB
tel: 01235 827827
fax: 01235 400401
e-mail: education@bookpoint.co.uk
Lines are open 9.00 a.m.–5.00 p.m., Monday to Saturday, with a 24-hour message answering service. You can also order through the Philip Allan website: www.philipallan.co.uk

ISBN 978-1-4718-0877-7

First printed 2014
Impression number 5 4 3 2 1
Year 2017 2016 2015 2014

Cover photo: C/Fotolia

Typeset by Integra Software Services Pvt. Ltd, Pondicherry, India

Printed in Dubai

Hachette UK's policy is to use papers that are natural, renewable and recyclable products and made from wood grown in sustainable forests. The logging and manufacturing processes are expected to conform to the environmental regulations of the country of origin.

P2301

Contents

Content Guidance

What is a constitution and what do constitutions do? • Why is the American constitution so important? • Constitutional change • The strengths and weaknesses of the codified American constitution • The US constitution and federalism • The protection of rights in the US constitution • Some comparisons with the UK constitution

Why is the US Congress so powerful? • Bicameralism • Congress and legislation • Congressional oversight • How important is the role of party in Congress? • Congress and representation • Members of Congress and constituency service • How representative are members of Congress? • Comparisons with the bicameral Westminster Parliament

What are the constitutional powers of the American president? • How have presidential roles developed since the constitution was written? • The presidency since the 1930s • Presidential resources • The role of the federal bureaucracy • Comparisons with the UK executive

Why is the Supreme Court so important in the US system of government? • What is judicial review? • How are Supreme Court justices appointed? • Judicial independence • Judicial philosophy • The protection of rights by the Supreme Court • What are the main constraints on the power of the Supreme Court? • The Supreme Court: a 'political' or 'judicial' body? • Comparisons with the UK judiciary

Questions & Answers

Getting the most from this book

Questions & Answers

Exam-style questions

Examiner comments on the questions
Tips on what you need to do to gain full marks, indicated by the icon ⓔ.

Sample student answers
Practise the questions, then look at the student answers that follow each question.

Examiner commentary on sample student answers
Find out how many marks each answer would be awarded in the exam and then read the examiner comments (preceded by the icon ⓔ) following each student answer. Annotations that link back to points made in the student answers show exactly how and where marks are gained or lost.

AQA A2 Government & Politics

About this book

This guide has been written to help students opting for AQA Unit 4A, The Government of the USA, to prepare more effectively. Its aim is to provide students with a clear outline of the way in which the unit is structured and examined, as well as a summary of the content for each part of the unit.

The Content Guidance section looks at the core content of the unit, focusing on the four areas covered in the specification, including key concepts and theories, knowledge checks and examiner tips. The Questions and Answers section includes information on the structure of the examination, information on assessment and examination advice.

Specification at a glance

The constitutional framework of US government

Key concepts	Content and amplification
• Fundamental law • Codified constitution • Limited government • Flexibility/rigidity • Federalism • Decentralisation and states' rights • Constitutional sovereignty • Entrenched rights • Constitutional interpretation	• The nature and significance of the US constitution and the framework of government that it lays down • The importance of the constitutional principles of the separation of powers and checks and balances to the operation of government and the way that these apply in practice today • The significance of the Bill of Rights • The amendment process • The federal system of government and its implications • The relationship between the federal government and the states • Constitutional change and its causes and effects • Debates concerning the importance of the US constitution to the working of US government today • The Supreme Court and the constitution • Comparisons with the UK's uncodified constitution and unitary system to illustrate arguments

The legislative branch of government: US Congress

Key concepts	Content and amplification
• Bicameralism • Gridlock • Presidential veto and congressional override • Impeachment • Advice and consent powers • Pork barrelling • Filibuster	• The constitutional role and power(s) of the US Congress • The composition of Congress and the different terms of office • The differences between the House and the Senate and the relationship between the two houses • Debates concerning the functions, powers and effectiveness of Congress in legislation, oversight and the power of the purse • The importance of both the party system and the committee system within Congress • The representative role of senators and representatives • Debates concerning the social composition of Congress • The relationship of Congress with the executive branch and the Supreme Court • Comparisons with the Westminster Parliament to illustrate arguments

Key concepts	Content and amplification
• Presidential executive • Imperial presidency • Imperilled presidency • Veto • Power to persuade • Bureaucratic power • Iron triangles • Spoils system • Clientelism	• The constitution and the executive branch of government • Debates concerning presidential power, both formal and informal, and the ability to actually exercise it in both domestic and foreign policy • Limitations and constraints on executive power from the constitution, Congress and the Supreme Court • Debates concerning the main determinants of presidential–congressional relations. The ebb and flow of power • The nature of the exercise of power within the executive branch • Debates concerning the relative power and influence of the cabinet and the Executive Office of the President • The role of the federal bureaucracy and the federal agencies • Comparisons with the UK executive to illustrate arguments

The judicial branch of government: the Supreme Court

Key concepts	Content and amplification
• Constitutional interpretation • Judicial review • Original intent • Judicial activism and restraint • Strict and loose constructionism • Judicial power • Entrenched rights	• The constitutional role of the Supreme Court and the nature of judicial power • The Supreme Court's role as guardian of the constitution through constitutional interpretation • The Supreme Court's power of judicial review since 1803 • Debates and controversies surrounding the selection and appointment process of Supreme Court justices • The political significance of the Supreme Court and the impact of its landmark judgements • The protection of citizens' rights by the Supreme Court • The relationship of the Supreme Court with the other branches of government • Comparison with the senior judiciary in the UK to illustrate arguments

You can get a copy of the AQA specification through the website www.aqa.org.uk. This includes sample questions, mark schemes and the generic assessment criteria.

How to do well in Unit 4A

It is important to recognise that A2 units are more demanding than AS units. Read widely around the subject to broaden and deepen your knowledge of American government. This should include:

- UK and US quality newspapers and websites
- up-to-date textbooks on American government and politics
- articles in *Politics Review* that are focused on specific topics
- current affairs journals such as *Time* or *Newsweek* and *The Economist* (which includes an excellent American Survey section)
- A. J. Bennett's *US Government and Politics Annual Survey*, published by Philip Allan

Watch the television news regularly to update your notes. Record significant developments or events in American government. Keep an organised file from the beginning of your course. Review your notes on a regular basis, learning as you go along and avoiding last-minute panics.

Content Guidance

This section of the guide aims to address the key areas of content of the four sections of the AQA Unit 4A specification. It focuses on the main theories, issues and debates in these four areas and contains the key concepts that you need to know and understand as well as knowledge checks and examiner tips. While making no claim to cover every possible aspect of the four specification areas in detail, the content guidance aims to provide concise but thorough coverage of the core topics. This material is best used as the basis for further study and your own independent research.

The constitutional framework of US government

The starting point for the study of the government of the United States of America is the US constitution. The original document, written in Philadelphia in 1787 by the Founding Fathers, in seven articles of over 7,000 words, is the oldest written constitution. A product of the revolutionary war of independence and struggle against the tyranny of colonial rule, its provisions were influenced by the writings of political theorists such as Locke and Montesquieu. It represented a sharp turn in US history and the beginning of the world's first modern democracy.

The US constitution is as important to the understanding of the operation of US government today as it was in the eighteenth century.

What is a constitution and what do constitutions do?

A constitution is an authoritative set of rules that seeks to establish the role, powers and functions of the institutions of government (legislative, executive and judicial), regulate the relationships between them and define the relationship between the state and its citizens. A constitution can be both written and unwritten, and codified or uncodified.

Why is the American constitution so important?

- It is the supreme law of the USA. Constitutional law is fundamental law, providing the rules that govern the government.
- It is the source of, but also a limitation on, the power of government.
- It provides for governments to have enough power to be strong and effective, while at the same time protecting the individual liberties of citizens against the abuse of that power.

fundamental law and constitutional sovereignty The constitution provides the fundamental constitutional law of the United States. It is also in many senses the 'rules of the game' for US politics. Unlike the UK, where Parliament is the ultimate source of authority, a concept called parliamentary sovereignty, in the USA it is the constitution, hence we refer to constitutional sovereignty.

Meaning more than simply 'written', a codified constitution is one where rules and principles are codified into a single document containing the nation's constitutional arrangements. The US constitution is codified into one document of 7,000 words in 7 articles and 27 amendments, unlike the UK constitution, which lacks a single codified document but derives from both written and unwritten sources.

limited government
Linked to the framers' view that 'the government is best that governs least', the term applies to limitations placed on the power of government to avoid the concentrated power and potential tyranny they feared. Together with constitutional devices like the separation of powers, checks and balances, federalism and entrenched rights protecting the liberties of citizens, limited government is deeply established in US political culture.

- It balances the need for a strong federal government with the need to give autonomy to the states.
- It is codified in a single document and entrenched.

Key principles

There were four main provisions laid down in the constitution:

1 **Representative and accountable government** through the provision of fixed-term elections held every 4 years for the president and every 2 years for the House of Representatives. (The Senate was not directly elected until 1913.)
2 The **separation of powers**, with the three branches of government (legislative, executive and judicial) separated through the first three articles of the constitution. The powers of the each branch were then subject to checks and balances by the other two bodies.
3 A **federal structure** of government, with power divided between the federal government in Washington and the individual states.
4 There was to be limited government, with citizens given inalienable and entrenched rights in the Bill of Rights (the first ten amendments), added in 1791.

Although there have been some formal amendments since 1791, these principles still form the basis of the operation of US government today. They are therefore crucial to the understanding of the workings of the executive, legislature and judiciary in the USA.

The separation of powers

The principle was adopted from the writings of Montesquieu in 1748. Montesquieu stressed the need to avoid tyranny by fragmenting the power of government through the device of the separation of powers. The theory is that each of the functions of government (passing laws, executing laws and adjudicating on laws) should be exercised by a different branch:

- the legislature (Article 1, Congress)
- the executive (Article 2, President)
- the judiciary (Article 3, Supreme Court)

The underlying aim was to avoid tyranny and to protect liberty. Power would not be concentrated in one branch of government but separated between the branches.

The theory implies independence of the branches of government. It implies that there should be a separation of personnel, with no overlap between the three branches. This is why Barack Obama and John Kerry, for example, had to give up their Senate seats when becoming president and secretary of state.

However, the theory also implies the *interdependence* of the branches of government through the associated checks and balances placed on each of them, particularly the legislative and executive branches, to prevent any one from becoming too powerful. This is why American political scientist Richard Neustadt described the American system not as a 'separation of powers' (which would mean that nothing could ever work) but as 'separate institutions sharing powers', where power is very difficult to exercise but where the branches have to work together to get things done.

An incomplete separation

This separation of personnel is, however, not absolute and you should be aware of a couple of overlaps:

- The vice-president (part of the executive) is also officially president of the Senate and can cast a tie-breaking vote. Dick Cheney used this power eight times between 2001 and 2009.
- The president can issue presidential pardons to convicted offenders (a judicial function).

Checks and balances in the USA

The following are some examples of the checks and balances in the system:

- Congress has legislative power but this power is checked by the presidential veto.
- The presidential veto is checked by the use of a congressional override with a two-thirds majority in both houses of Congress.
- The Supreme Court can decide that laws (and actions) are unconstitutional through its power of judicial review, which it 'discovered' in the 1803 *Marbury* v *Madison* case.
- The president is the commander-in-chief of the armed forces but only Congress can declare (and fund) war.
- Presidential appointments need to be confirmed and presidential treaties need to be ratified with the 'advice and consent' of the Senate.

So the branches of US government can and do constrain each other's power.

Criticisms

It has been argued that the system offers an 'invitation to struggle', to the executive and legislative branches in particular, and can be a recipe for institutional gridlock, with little being achieved as a result of dysfunctional power struggles between the branches. This is particularly the case when there is **divided government** in Washington: for example, after the elections of 2010 and 2012 with the branches controlled by different parties (encouraged by the constitutional provision of staggered elections). It is likely that this was the intention of the Founding Fathers, who wished, above all, to restrain the exercise of power and avoid its concentration in the executive branch. Many have argued that this has led to weak government, inertia and difficulty in making decisions, especially controversial ones such as the inability to reach consensus when setting the federal budget in 2012–13. This resulted in the temporary shutdown of the federal government in October 2013.

An alternative argument, however, is that the system means that the branches of government *must* work cooperatively for anything to be done, and that this leads to more consensus seeking, negotiation, bargaining and compromise to achieve common goals and solutions. The growth in partisanship and polarisation of the two parties over the past 20 years has, however, made this increasingly difficult.

Constitutional change

A key debate surrounding the role of a constitution in the political life of a nation is how easily it can adapt to changing circumstances and conditions. Put simply,

---

congressional override As part of the constitutional checks and balances, Congress can override a presidential regular veto (but not a pocket veto) on legislation by a two-thirds majority passed in both houses. This is difficult to achieve and it is extremely rare to gain the numbers necessary. Clinton had 2 of his 36 vetoes and G. W. Bush had 4 of his 11 vetoes successfully overridden. The rest of the vetoes were sustained.

Knowledge check 1

Explain the principle of the separation of powers.

Knowledge check 2

Why is it more accurate to describe the USA as having 'separated institutions sharing powers' than a 'separation of powers'?

Knowledge check 3

Explain the principle of checks and balances.

Examiner tip

Be prepared both to defend and to criticise the separation of powers and checks and balances, particularly in modern conditions of 'big' government, and to give reasons for criticisms of institutional gridlock, on the one hand, but also the benefits of greater consensus and compromise that must be sought, on the other.

---

this relates to arguments about whether constitutions are rigid or flexible, easy or difficult to change. The reality is that *all* constitutions, whether codified or not, have some degree of both rigidity *and* flexibility.

The Founding Fathers recognised the need to safeguard constitutional rules from the 'whims' of 'temporary' governments and, although 'ordinary law' is made in Congress (subject to judicial review by the Supreme Court since 1803), the constitution itself was deliberately made difficult to change. Nevertheless, it would not be correct to describe it as rigid; indeed it has been described as a living document, still relevant today.

How can the US constitution be changed?

Change through the formal amendment process (Article 5)

Formal constitutional amendment is a tortuous process, requiring supermajorities of at least two-thirds of the vote in *both* houses of Congress, followed by ratification by three-quarters of the state legislatures (meaning 13 states could block any constitutional change).

This process entails a prolonged period of debate and demands a clear consensus in favour of change, thus avoiding hasty decisions made without adequate thought. As a result, there have been only 27 amendments to the constitution since it was written. This number includes the first ten amendments, the Bill of Rights, ratified in 1791.

Most proposed amendments fail to attract the required support. Examples include:
- a balanced budget amendment — this would never pass in Congress
- an equal rights amendment — this failed to get the required states' vote
- making abortion, same-sex marriage or flag burning unconstitutional

Examples of successful constitutional amendments include:
- the civil rights amendments following the Civil War (13th, 14th and 15th Amendments)
- direct election for the Senate (17th Amendment, 1913)
- amendments to extend voting rights — to women (19th Amendment, 1921) and to age 18 (26th Amendment, 1971)
- two-term presidency (22nd Amendment, 1951)

The other way of getting a formal change to the constitution is through the calling of a constitutional convention by two-thirds of the states. This method has never been used.

Change through Supreme Court interpretation

'We are under a Constitution, but the Constitution is what the judges say it is.' (Chief Justice Hughes, 1909)

The US constitution is a short document containing some vague language. It is likely that the Founding Fathers intended it to be open to interpretation in future times and not be regarded as a tablet of stone forever set in eighteenth-century conditions. The amendments are also written in general rather than specific language: for example, the 14th Amendment's 'equal protection of the laws' and the 8th Amendment's banning of 'cruel and unusual' punishment.

The interpretation of the meaning of the words of the constitution and its amendments is the function of the Supreme Court, through the cases brought before it. The words themselves do not change (they are simply 'words on paper'), but their meaning is subject to revision and updating through judicial interpretation. Such revisions are referred to as informal 'interpretative amendments' rather than formal changes through amendment.

The same phrases in the constitution may be interpreted differently at different times and in different circumstances; for example, the phrase 'equal protection of the laws' in the 14th Amendment was interpreted one way in the *Plessy* v *Ferguson* case of 1896, but very differently in the *Brown* v *Board of Education of Topeka* case in 1954. The growth of presidential powers from the 1930s and the shift of authority from state to federal government are similarly the result of Supreme Court interpretation of the constitution.

The constitution is therefore more flexible and less rigid than is commonly thought. US government has been able to evolve and adapt in response to new challenges and demands that have arisen through changing conditions and circumstances, such as civil war, great depression, foreign wars including the 'war on terror', Watergate and presidential impeachment.

Change through developing conventions

All constitutions, including the American, are a blend of both written and unwritten rules. The US constitution refers to broad principles only and lays down a loose framework of government. As a result, many of the ways in which government in the USA today actually works in practice are not in the constitution and have no constitutional status. Examples include:

- the existence and workings of the cabinet, the Executive Office of the President (EXOP) and the federal bureaucracy
- the huge power of the congressional committees, and the Supreme Court's power of judicial review, neither of which is constitutionally derived

When the US constitution was written in 1787, it was for a country with 3 million inhabitants in 13 states, facing relatively simple issues that needed to be resolved. It is that same document, plus amendments, which is now providing the framework of government for a world superpower, a country of over 313 million inhabitants in 50 states, facing highly complex economic, social and foreign policy issues unimagined in the eighteenth century. The US constitution has been described as 'brilliantly adaptive' despite its codified nature, as it has changed and evolved to meet these new conditions. It can be judged by how well it has stood the test of time.

The strengths and weaknesses of the codified American constitution

Major strengths

- Sovereignty comes from the constitution and its major principles are entrenched, safe from interference from the whims of governments, which come and go. It provides a sense of stability and continuity.

judicial interpretation
The Supreme Court is the final arbiter of the constitution, as Article 3 stated that its judicial power extended to 'all cases arising under this Constitution', further extended after *Marbury* v *Madison* established the principle of judicial review. This power is used to adjudicate disputes between the branches and layers of government and citizens and state, so its vague wording can be interpreted differently over time, linking to constitutional flexibility.

Knowledge check 5

Explain why amendments such as the 8th and the 14th often cause controversy.

Examiner tip
Note that constitutional change can occur through Supreme Court interpretation of the document in cases brought before it, as well as by 'conventions' evolving over the years in the custom and practice of government. Examples of all types of constitutional change should be known for use as examples.

- It constrains the exercise of power by the different branches of government, thus avoiding the development of an 'elective dictatorship' or 'executive dominance'.
- Individual liberties, such as freedom of expression, are entrenched and widely known and supported.
- It contains the flexibility to be amended in response to changing political conditions.
- Its provisions are safeguarded by the independent Supreme Court.
- There is no pressure for change from the American people, only a debate often over how the constitution should be interpreted in controversial areas.

Major weaknesses

- It is more rigid than the uncodified UK constitution and is therefore less easily adapted, despite changing conditions (for example, the criticisms made of the 2nd Amendment, the right to bear arms).
- Many argue that too much power is given to the unelected and unaccountable Supreme Court judges.
- It can be argued that the growth of presidential and federal power has not been sufficiently constrained, and that constitutional rights and states' rights are therefore not sufficiently protected.
- The difficulties of governing in a separated and checked-and-balanced system can result in gridlock, where difficult but necessary decisions are hard to make and carry out. This is especially true in times of 'divided government' when one party controls the White House and the other controls all or part of Congress.
- The 2-year terms for congressmen/women makes for a situation of almost constant campaigning and increased costs.

The constitution is the underlying feature of all the following pages in this section of the guide and of most examination questions. You are highly advised to read it before attempting any serious study of US government.

The US constitution and federalism

Constitutions can be federal or unitary. The origins of the US constitution as a federal constitution lay in the Articles of Confederation (which governed the USA from 1781 to 1788) and in the debates that took place over where power should be located. The key issue was whether power should be with the new federal (central) government or whether it should be with the individual states.

Like the separation of powers in the branches of government, federalism fragments power between the layers of government and avoids its concentration. It has, however, led to power struggles and controversy over where the balance of power should lie.

What is federalism?

Federalism involves the division of power between the national (federal) government and the 50 individual states. It is the decentralisation of power, with power dispersed between the two levels. It is sometimes referred to as *dual sovereignty*, as each of the 50 states also has its own government structured around:
- a state constitution
- a state governor (executive)

Knowledge check 6

Why would it be incorrect to describe the US constitution as 'rigid'?

Knowledge check 7

How does the constitution fragment power?

federalism A principle relating to the division of power between the federal and state governments, as the framers sought a balance between a strong central government and the power of the previously independent states. Each level of government has its own area of substantive jurisdiction, but the balance of power between them is not fixed, changing through Supreme Court interpretation of the vague words of the constitution in this area.

- a bicameral state House and Senate (legislature) — except Nebraska, which has a unicameral legislature
- a state Supreme Court (judiciary)

Federalism, in the words of Madison, avoids 'the danger of too much power in too few hands', thus helping to preserve freedom and adding another set of checks and balances on the exercise of political power.

The key benefit of federalism is that it maintains national unity while at the same time preserving state diversity. It also means, however, that American citizens are subject to two sets of laws that act directly upon them. What is legal in one state may be illegal in another. This currently applies, for example, to gay marriage, which is only legal in a minority of states.

What does the constitution say about federalism?

There is no mention of the word 'federalism' in the US constitution, which was a compromise between the federalists, who wanted a strong national government, and the anti-federalists, who wanted power to lie with the individual states. However:

- The constitution gives the states equal representation in the Senate (two per state).
- The constitution specifies that an amendment can pass only with the agreement of three-quarters of the states.
- The 10th Amendment guarantees states' rights through the reserved powers (see below).

How does federalism work?

The constitution gives both the federal and the state governments guaranteed powers and their own areas of authority, thus inviting a second struggle between the two layers of government, as well as between the branches within them. There have been numerous developments in federalism since the constitution was written in 1787:

- The **enumerated powers** (Article 1) state that the federal Congress can legislate on defence, currency and naturalisation of citizens, regulate interstate commerce and provide for the 'common defense'.
- The **inherent powers**, including responsibility for foreign relations and waging war, are also given to the federal government.
- The **implied powers** are not explicit but are shown in the constitution's wording: for example, that Congress can make laws that are 'necessary and proper' for exercising the enumerated powers and to provide for 'the general welfare' — both clauses linking to several Supreme Court cases (including the constitutionality of healthcare provisions passed by Congress in 2009), determining their precise meaning in a modern context.
- In the *McCulloch v Maryland* (1819) case, the Supreme Court established the supremacy of the federal government and Congress over state governments through its interpretation of the 'necessary and proper' clause over the issue of a national bank. The court's interpretation paved the way for later rulings upholding federal over state power.
- The **16th Amendment** in 1913 allowed for a federal income tax to be levied by the federal government across all the states. This was a watershed in the development of federalism and federal government control of taxing and spending for federal policies and the subsequent dependence of the states on federal finance.

Knowledge check 8

Why is the 16th Amendment important to understanding federal–state relations?

- The **reserved powers** are those left to the states and guaranteed by the 10th Amendment. They form the basis of states' rights, such as law enforcement and electoral law, and explain the diversity of laws in different states.
- The **concurrent powers** are those shared by both state and federal government, such as legislative power, taxation power, health, education and safety.

Phases of federalism

The parameters of federal and state power are not fixed and the nature of federal–state relations has developed and changed throughout US history. There have been several phases of federalism:

- **Dual federalism.** In simpler times before the 1930s New Deal, the federal and state governments were largely independent of each other, with clearly defined spheres of influence and power rarely overlapping. This is referred to as a 'layer-cake', with separate and distinct layers.
- **Cooperative federalism.** This came after the huge expansion of federal government intervention and regulation after the Great Depression and subsequent New Deal. The term refers to the partnership that evolved between the two levels of government, with the federal government assisting the states to cope with the new demands: a national crisis demanded a centralised response. This was also true of the period of the Great Society under Lyndon Johnson's administration of the 1960s, when money was given to the states but with strings attached, so there was more control by the federal government. This phase of federalism is sometimes referred to as a 'marble cake', with an inseparable mix of layers.
- **New federalism.** This came about as a result of the Republican presidencies of Nixon and Reagan, as a reaction against the growth of federal government power and its bureaucratic costs. New federalism emphasised states' rights, small government and 'getting government off the backs of the people'. Both Republican administrations provided block grants to the states to spend as they wished (rather than having the states be directed in their spending by the requirements of the federal government through categorical grants). This continued into the presidency of Clinton, who famously declared that the 'era of big government is over' after the Republican takeover of Congress in 1994.
- The George W. Bush presidency started with a philosophy of small government and, Bush being an ex-governor, a commitment to states' rights. However, the demands of the war on terror, homeland security, the aftermath of Hurricane Katrina, and the No Child Left Behind Act resulted in more federal government intervention than would normally be seen in a Republican administration. This has continued under the Obama administration with one-third of the $787 billion stimulus going to the states but most of it with specified federally directed spending.

What are the main advantages of federalism?

- It provides an additional set of checks and balances on the exercise of power, guarding against an over-powerful central government.
- It allows for the diversity and traditions of the 50 states to be reflected
- It provides opportunities for citizens to be politically involved at local level.
- The states can be training grounds for national leadership. George W. Bush was the governor of Texas, Obama was a state senator and then US senator for Illinois, and his rival in 2012, Mitt Romney, had been governor of Massachusetts.

- States can show both autonomy and initiative. They can even be laboratories for experimental new policies to see if they work, for example caps on carbon emissions in New York and California or the innovative use of education vouchers in Wisconsin.

What are the main disadvantages of federalism?

- Too much fragmentation of government can lead to gridlock. The states can also be obstructive and refuse to conform, for example the refusal of the southern states to de-segregate after the Brown decision in 1954, claiming that states' rights allowed them to refuse.
- The variety of state laws on, for example, abortion, gun ownership and the death penalty causes confusion and a lack of cohesion in the country.
- There are significant economic inequalities between rich and poor states, such as Connecticut and Louisiana, and variable provisions for citizens, which only the federal government has the resources to equalise.
- There is democratic overload, with too many elective offices at state level and, therefore, too many elections.

How federal is the USA in reality?

There is no doubt that the power of central government has expanded considerably from the 1930s onwards, but there still remain some areas where states have retained their power. This means that there can still be considerable variation between states. Some of the main differences that can be found between states include:

- the death penalty (still legal in 32 states)
- some aspects of elections, for example whether to have open or closed primaries
- local sales tax
- regulations concerning gambling and the sale of alcohol (though since 1988 the USA has had a national minimum drinking age set at 21 — a good example of the inter-relationship between federal and state laws)

The protection of rights in the US constitution

The Founding Fathers were concerned above all to protect the rights and liberties of citizens under the new constitution. Jefferson's Declaration of Independence focused on the 'inalienable rights' of the people, but it is a matter for debate how well the freedoms of US citizens today are protected.

The Bill of Rights

These first ten amendments to the constitution were ratified by the states in 1791 and have remained as they were since that date. They are **entrenched** and guaranteed constitutional rights:

- The **1st Amendment** protects freedom of religion, the press, speech and assembly. It begins 'Congress shall make no law' abridging these freedoms. Freedom of speech has been interpreted as the freedom to burn the flag and to spend money to support political views as in the *Citizens United* v *FEC* case in 2010.
- The **2nd Amendment** protects the right to bear arms. This remains controversial but has been upheld in the 2009 *DC* v *Heller* case.

Knowledge check 10

Why do liberals favour federal government power and conservatives favour giving more power to the states?

Knowledge check 11

Why are states sometimes described as 'laboratories of experiment'?

Examiner tip
There is no agreement about the federal–state relationship or where power should reside. Be aware of the key arguments in debates over the advantages and disadvantages of a federal system and controversies that can arise between the federal government and the states, such as those over immigration law in Arizona.

entrenched rights
Unlike in the UK where Parliament can legislate to take away rights, the USA has inalienable rights entrenched in the Bill of Rights and subsequent amendments, which cannot be infringed. Designed as protection from the tyranny of over-powerful government, they guarantee the key liberties of US citizens. Protected (usually) by the Supreme Court, laws may be struck down if they contradict the rights guaranteed in the amendments.

- The **3rd Amendment** protects the rights of property owners, including a broader protection of privacy.
- The **4th Amendment** guarantees freedom from unreasonable searches and seizures of persons and property.
- The **5th Amendment** guarantees the rights of the accused and includes the 'due process clause', whereby no person shall be deprived of life, liberty or property without due process of law. It also protects the right to silence in a court of law.
- The **6th Amendment** sets out rights for those standing trial and protects against arbitrary arrest and imprisonment. It has been used to challenge aspects of holding detainees at Guantánamo Bay.
- The **7th Amendment** deals mainly with civil law suits.
- The **8th Amendment** bans 'cruel and unusual punishment', which is controversial, given the existence of the death penalty in many states. It has, however, been used to place restrictions on imposing the death penalty, such as limiting it to over 18s and solely for murder cases.
- The **9th Amendment** is concerned with the rights 'reserved to the people' and states that people may have other rights not found in the Bill of Rights. It has been used in many privacy cases, including *Roe* v *Wade*.
- The **10th Amendment** is concerned with the rights reserved to the states.

Rights are also protected by several of the other constitutional amendments, such as the 14th Amendment with its reference to the 'equal protection of the laws'.

For the role of the Supreme Court in protecting constitutional rights through constitutional interpretation and judicial review, see pp. 43–44. In general, 'activist' courts protect and extend rights through interpretation, while courts that are more 'restrained' are less likely to do so.

It is important to note the existence of a strong 'rights culture' in the USA, with most Americans knowing their rights and understanding that the courts are there to protect them.

However, 'words on paper' do not always guarantee that these rights will be applied at all times and under all conditions. There are many instances in US history where rights have not been fully protected and applied:

- the denial of voting rights and civil rights to black Americans after the 14th and 15th Amendments, when segregation and Jim Crow laws prevailed in the southern states
- the internment (imprisonment without trial) of Japanese Americans during the Second World War
- the passage of the Patriot Act, a raft of anti-terrorism measures such as wire tapping and electronic surveillance, passed by Congress after 9/11 — many argued such measures undermined constitutional rights, but they were not declared 'unconstitutional' by the Supreme Court
- the existence of Guantánamo Bay camp, where prisoners were detained without habeas corpus rights or 'due process of law' as a result of the so-called war on terror

It can therefore be argued that what happens to rights, despite constitutional protection, depends on the climate, circumstances and events of the times.

Examiner tip

Knowledge of the Bill of Rights and other important constitutional amendments is essential to many questions and their guaranteed provisions to the American people should be known, as well as important Supreme Court cases that have arisen over their interpretation.

Knowledge check 12

Why has the Patriot Act been criticised?

Examiner tip

Despite entrenched rights and a strong 'rights culture' there are times when rights have been denied or not applied, and examples should be known of some of these to present a balanced argument on whether citizens' rights have (or not) been adequately protected.

Some comparisons with the UK constitution

- There is no single, authoritative, codified document that is *the* constitution. However, the UK constitution cannot be described as unwritten, as there are many written elements to it.
- Traditionally, the main principle of the UK constitution is parliamentary sovereignty, as opposed to the constitutional sovereignty found in the USA. The impact of the European Convention on Human Rights and also of EU law have, however, somewhat weakened this principle.
- There is a fusion of powers in the UK system of government, with the executive being drawn from the legislature and also responsible to it. As a result, there are fewer checks and balances in the UK system, leading to criticisms of 'elective dictatorship' and 'executive dominance', although an advantage is that a strong government can carry out its electoral mandate without gridlock, and quickly in the event of a crisis.
- The UK constitution is often described as flexible because it can easily be changed through a law passed by a simple majority in parliament. This means it is easily adaptable to changing conditions and circumstances.
- There is a unitary rather than a federal system of government. Power is centralised and concentrated in the sovereign Westminster Parliament, although Parliament can and has devolved some of its power.
- Rights are not entrenched or guaranteed in the UK in quite the same way.

After studying this topic you should be able to:

- Understand the circumstances surrounding the writing of the US constitution and its crucial importance to understanding the workings of US government today.
- Understand the key principles underpinning the way government works, such as the separation of powers and checks and balances, leading to fragmentation of the power of American government.
- Know the debates over the applicability of the key constitutional principles to the realities of government in the 21st century.
- Explain processes of constitutional change including amendment, interpretation and developing usage, showing how and why the constitution today differs from the original 1787 document.
- Show knowledge of constitutional change proposed but never brought about, and the reasons why.
- Identify the major strengths and weaknesses of the sovereign US constitution.

- Explain the nature of American federalism and the division of power and sovereignty between the federal government and the states.
- Show how federalism works in practice, developing since 1787 through constitutional amendment, constitutional interpretation and changing practice.
- Explain reasons for different phases of federalism and the links to changing political and economic conditions and Republican and Democratic ideology.
- Identify the main advantages and disadvantages of US federalism.
- Identify and explain the nature of entrenched rights, especially in the Bill of Rights, and subsequent amendments such as the 14th.
- Understand that, despite entrenchment, there are times when rights have not been fully protected because of the circumstances of the time.
- Make appropriate and relevant comparisons with the uncodified UK constitution.

Summary

The legislative branch of government: US Congress

The US Congress is the legislative branch of the federal government and its role is described in Article 1 of the constitution. This shows the clear intention of the framers of the constitution that Congress was to have a dominant role. The constitution gives all legislative power to Congress to make laws for the USA, although today, because of vastly changed conditions, it tends to follow a presidential agenda.

Congress may be the most powerful legislature in the world, but it operates under a codified constitution, with separated powers from the other branches of government and checks and balances to limit its powers. Its legislative powers are also constrained by the Bill of Rights, with the 1st Amendment starting 'Congress shall make no law', as befits the framers' desire for limited government.

Congress has been described as a policy-making rather than a policy-influencing legislature. This is unusual, as most modern legislatures are executive dominated.

Why is the US Congress so powerful?

- It is independent from the executive branch of government and cannot be controlled by it. Congress can and does ignore or over-rule presidential policies.
- It controls the purse-strings, a particular function of the House of Representatives.
- It is the representative assembly of the USA — the voice of the people.
- It has many constitutional powers, both enumerated and implied.

Bicameralism

Congress is made up of two different but equally powerful houses, the **House of Representatives** and the **Senate**. The constitution deliberately created two houses that would check and balance each other and respond in different ways to different constituencies and pressures. This is known as bicameralism.

The difference in representation between the House and the Senate

- The House of Representatives represents districts within states.
- There are 435 districts and they are apportioned according to the population of the state: the more populous the state, the greater the number of districts within it. California the state with the largest population has 53 districts; in small states with low populations, like South Dakota, the whole state is one district.
- The allocation of districts to states may alter after every census (the last was in 2010), as states can gain or lose districts according to population change. This is known as re-apportionment. This in turn leads to the need to redraw the boundaries of districts. This re-districting is usually done by partisan state legislatures and is often controversial because of gerrymandering (altering the boundaries for party advantage).

Knowledge check 13

Explain why Congress is described as a 'policy-making' rather than 'policy-influencing' legislature.

Examiner tip

Always be able to explain why Congress is, and was intended to be, so powerful in US government, giving examples of both its constitutional power(s) and the constraints on the exercise of its power because of the constitutional checks and balances.

bicameralism The framers deliberately created a Congress of two chambers, with different terms of office, representation and powers, as additional checks and balances against the concentration of power and potential tyranny. Although they must mainly work together to get things done, they remain two different houses, and the outcomes of their deliberations will be different as they represent different electorates, have different roles and exercise different powers.

By contrast:
- The Senate represents whole states.
- Because of the Connecticut Compromise, there is equal representation of the states, with two senators per state regardless of size or population. However, this representation has been criticised as unfair because, for example, Wyoming (population around 580,000) has the same Senate representation as California (population over 38 million).

Different terms of office

- The House of Representatives is elected for 2-year terms of office. The intention was to keep representatives highly responsive to the wishes of the people, and the effect of these very short terms does make re-election their prime motivating force.
- The House is a more parochial chamber than the Senate, dominated by the constituency interests of the 'folks back home', and the voting record of most House members reflects the views and interests of their district.
- Senators are elected for 6-year terms, but elections for the Senate are staggered, with a third of the senators up for re-election every 2 years in both mid-term and presidential elections.
- The intention was that senators would be more like national statesmen, above the fray, with a more long-term view on political issues compared to their more populist counterparts in the House.
- The longer terms of the senators protect them from the populist 'whims of the day', and the fact that they represent states with a huge diversity of interests within them means that they are less parochial than the House Representatives in their voting.

Different status and prestige

It is generally held that the Senate is the more prestigious and sought-after chamber. There are a number of reasons for this:
- Being a senator involves being part of a more elite and select group, and with only 100 members there is more opportunity to sit on and even chair important committees. A congressman/woman is only one of 435 members.
- A senator's term is longer, meaning that there is less of a focus on re-election and greater job security.
- Congressmen/women can be threatened by partisan re-districting (gerry-mandering) every 10 years.
- The Senate has more exclusive powers as discussed below.
- A senator is likely to have a higher profile within a state and possibly nationally.
- The Senate is a much better 'talent pool' for executive office. Many presidents and vice-presidents have come up from the Senate including Obama and Biden. By contrast, very few have reached the White House directly from the House.
- Many senators have previously served as congressmen/women, but virtually none have made the journey the other way.

The constitutional powers of the House and the Senate

The House and the Senate share some powers — these are termed **concurrent powers** — but in other areas one chamber may exercise sole powers. These are known as **exclusive powers**.

> ### Knowledge check 14
> Explain the importance of the 'folks back home' to members of the House of Representatives.

> **presidential veto**
> A bill can be significantly amended by Congress before reaching the president's desk for signing into law, which may mean that the president will use his veto power to reject the entire bill. In conditions of divided government, the veto may be used more frequently to kill legislation passed against the president's agenda, and Congress may attempt to override the veto.

impeachment process
Impeachment is a rare congressional procedure involving formal accusation of wrongdoing by the House, which draws up the Articles of Impeachment (for personal not policy failures), with the Senate trying and convicting if a two-thirds majority agrees. Impeachment is the only way a president can be removed from office by Congress.

advice and consent powers The exclusive confirmation power of the Senate gives it power over the president's choice of executive branch members, Supreme Court justices and the federal judiciary. The ratification power allows oversight of the president's foreign policy through acceptance or rejection of negotiated treaties. These powers can be highly politicised, especially during periods of divided government.

Examiner tip
The House and Senate are very powerful but very different houses of the federal legislature, so make sure that you can always explain, with supporting examples, the main differences in their constitutional roles and powers, including their different representation and the differences in their legislative and oversight activities and outcomes.

Examples of concurrent powers

The constitution gives both houses:

- legislative power, including the power to override the presidential veto. The approval of both chambers is necessary for a bill to become law provided the president does not veto it.
- a role if the Electoral College is deadlocked after a presidential election
- scrutiny and oversight of the executive (government)
- the power to declare war
- the power to propose and pass constitutional amendments with a two-thirds majority
- a role in the impeachment process for 'high crimes and misdemeanors'. The House draws up the Articles of Impeachment and the Senate conducts the trial. Clinton was found not guilty at his impeachment trial in 1998 for perjury and obstruction of justice, and Nixon resigned before his likely impeachment in 1974 over Watergate.

Examples of exclusive powers

- The House of Representatives has the power to *originate* all money bills: for example, taxation is considered first in the House and then in the Senate. This gives the House the power to set the financial agenda and to control the purse strings of government through its powerful Ways and Means and Appropriations committees.
- The Senate has advice and consent powers, which means it has the power to **confirm** both presidential appointments and to **ratify** treaties:
  - **Confirmation** requires a simple majority vote for presidential appointments, such as Supreme Court justices, cabinet secretaries and ambassadors. The Senate has occasionally used these powers to deny a president's chosen nominee, for example the rejection of Reagan's choice of Bork for the Supreme Court in 1987. The most recent case though was over 20 years ago when the Senate rejected George Bush senior's choice of John Tower as defense secretary in 1989.
  - **Ratification** requires a two-thirds majority for treaties that have been negotiated by the president, who is chief diplomat, such as the Start Treaty ratified 71–26 in 2010. This gives the Senate some power over US foreign policy, although presidents have often resorted to the use of executive agreements to avoid the need for Senate ratification as it has rejected several negotiated treaties, such as Versailles in 1919 and SALT II in 1979. Most recently, in 2012, the Senate rejected a UN treaty on the rights of the disabled as conservative Republicans felt it could impinge on US sovereignty. The treaty fell five votes short of the necessary two-thirds majority.

Internal workings/procedures of the two houses

The House, chaired by the speaker, operates in a more formal and procedural way, with rules and limits on debate, as befits a chamber of 435 members.

The smaller Senate, chaired by the vice-president, who can vote only to break a tied vote, has procedures that are more informal and less rule-bound. The Senate has a tradition of unlimited debate, which gives rise to the infamous Senate filibuster.

Both House and Senate members are involved in:

- committees and subcommittees, both permanent and ad hoc
- pork barrelling, or 'bringing home the bacon', on spending bills
- 'log rolling' (vote trading on bills)
- coalition building to gain a majority of votes
- party and congressional caucuses

Party ties are still looser than they are at Westminster but have strengthened considerably over the past 30 years or so. This is in part because the two parties have become more polarised, and there are fewer moderates or centrists in both houses of Congress. Increasingly, legislators have to make sure their voting record accords with the views of the 'core' back home. It is local party activists who often play a big part in bringing about a defeat in the state primaries of a legislator they feel has been too 'moderate'. This happened in 2010 to Bob Bennett, a long-serving Republican senator for Utah, who had displeased local Tea Party supporters in his state.

Congress and legislation

The legislative process in Congress is frequently described as an obstacle course. Words associated with it are often negative, such as 'block', 'pigeon hole', 'veto'. Only a small fraction of bills introduced in Congress actually pass, usually less than 10%, and their failure is often unrelated to their merits, as in the case of healthcare reform in the 1990s or civil rights in the 1950s. Bills are especially vulnerable to defeat if they are controversial or opposed by powerful special interests. Furthermore, bills can be so significantly amended during the process that they become unrecognisable.

However, there *are* circumstances where bills have passed easily without being mired in the legislative labyrinth. An example is the Patriot Act, passed on a wave of patriotism and deference to the commander-in-chief after 9/11.

How is legislation initiated in the USA?

Legislation can only be initiated by a member of Congress (all members have legislative initiative), although most legislation today originates from a presidential agenda, with policy goals outlined in the president's State of the Union Address in January. This is followed by the presidential budget, which must be passed by both houses. However, although 'The president proposes, Congress disposes', all legislative proposals have to be introduced by a member of each house and must pass through both houses concurrently. There is no guarantee that legislation or the budget will pass in the way the president wishes it to, especially if there is divided government and presidential–congressional relations are poor, or if the houses have different party majorities, as seen after the 2010 mid-term elections.

Why is the legislative process so difficult?

The main reason for legislative failure is the number of *veto points* in both the House and the Senate where a bill may fail:

- House standing committee stage. Most bills die here as they are pigeon-holed by the chair, thus taken off the committee's agenda for the session.
- House subcommittee stage. Here the bill is examined in detail in hearings, with evidence taken from interested parties such as lobbyists or executive branch

pork barrelling In the legislative process, members of Congress try to gain constituency advantage by gaining 'pork' from the federal pork barrel through adding 'riders' or 'earmarks' to legislation, thus gaining federal funds for projects in their states and districts, such as road building or military bases. Pork barrelling links with home-style activities and incumbency advantage, but can lead to budget deficits and wasteful expenditure in the nation's economy.

Knowledge check 15

Explain the saying 'The president proposes, Congress disposes.'

officials. The bill can be significantly amended at this stage, as pork barrelling occurs, with numerous amendments or riders added to the bill to benefit constituents or special interests. The bill can fail at this stage.

- **House Rules Committee.** This powerful committee decides whether to give time to the bill on the floor of the House for debate. If this is not given, the bill dies.
- **Floor debate.** The amended bill is debated by the whole chamber. *Log rolling*, the exchange of votes and trading of favours by Representatives, may occur. Although there are whips and some ideological voting, there is relatively little party discipline and most members are more mindful of the folks back home or special interests in the roll-call voting at the end of the debate. The bill may fail on this floor vote.
- The bill follows similar stages in the Senate. It may fail in debate here due to a **filibuster**, the classic legislative delaying tactic whereby senators can individually or collectively 'talk out' a bill to defeat it. The filibuster is used because of the unlimited debate that is allowed and is a jealously guarded tactic employed by both parties when they are in a minority position in the Senate. Since 1975 it has been possible to end a filibuster through 'cloture', but this needs 60 votes, which are hard to gain, so defeat can come here. The bill can also fail in a vote at the end of Senate debate.
- Because the bill passes through both houses concurrently, it is likely that a different bill will emerge from both. The two different bills will need to be reconciled so an agreed bill can be sent to the White House. This is done through a Conference Committee, where senators and representatives try to reach a consensus through bargaining and compromise. If this cannot be done, then the bill dies.
- If reconciled, the bill needs to go back to both chambers for a final simple majority vote. It can still die here in either chamber.

Because of the separation of powers and checks and balances, the bill has to be signed by the president to become federal law. The president may veto the whole bill (he has no 'line-item veto' to turn down just the parts he doesn't like, as this was declared unconstitutional in 1998). If the veto is not overridden by a two-thirds vote in both houses and the veto is sustained, then the bill fails. During his first term, Obama only vetoed two bills, an all-time low. Neither veto was overridden. A president may 'pocket veto' a bill, which means he ignores it; if near the end of a congressional session, the bill will die. Even if the bill becomes law it can still be challenged in the courts, and the Supreme Court, using its power of judicial review, can declare it (or its parts) to be unconstitutional and therefore void.

Note how the federal shutdown in October 2013 was essentially because the House and Senate (controlled by different parties) could not agree on the budget. It was an example of the problems that can arise when the two parts of Congress (and the president) cannot agree.

Key points regarding the legislative process in Congress

- The separation of powers and numerous checks and balances make the process of law making difficult.
- The built-in tensions between the two houses and between Congress and president, as they are elected separately with few shared mandates, often lead to **gridlock**.

- The absence of strong party loyalty or effective party discipline of the sort seen in the UK Parliament, may lead to a lack of party unity on votes. Clinton's healthcare bill was defeated in 1994 even with a Democratic Congress. Obama struggled to gain support from conservative members of his own party for healthcare reform in 2009.
- Coalitions have to be built on each separate bill to construct a majority of votes. The president has only the power to persuade, through his Congressional Liaison Office.
- Congress blocks legislation on the president's agenda more effectively than it provides an alternative agenda of its own. Hence why Congress is sometimes known as the 'bastion of negation'.
- Members of Congress pork barrel in order to provide projects in their districts or states to help their re-election. They are less effective in providing a long-term or national perspective on policy or agreed solutions, unless there is a major event such as 9/11 or the 2008 banking crisis.

All these factors lead to criticisms of the legislative process in the US Congress.

However, in its defence, it does avoid the criticisms of executive dominance and elective dictatorship found in the UK. The process means there is a constant need to compromise and bargain to try to reach a consensus before the successful passage of federal law (although some may argue that such compromise eventually pleases no one).

Congressional oversight

This is the power of Congress to scrutinise and check the activities of the executive branch of government and hold it to account. Although the constitution does not explicitly give this power to Congress, it is exercised through:
- the legislative process
- Congress's control of the purse strings of government through taxation and spending
- the Senate's advice and consent powers (p. 20)
- the impeachment process (p. 20)

When the federal government was small, oversight was relatively unimportant. However, it is now one of the main functions of Congress in conditions of big and complex government.

Congressional committees

Oversight is done through the powerful permanent standing committees and is made even more effective by the huge number of congressional staff and resources devoted to oversight on Capitol Hill, such as the Congressional Budget Office.

All legislatures have committee systems within them, drawn from the larger body and with specific responsibilities. It is often said that the floors of the chambers are for debating, while the smaller committees are for working. As Woodrow Wilson said in 1884: 'Congressional government is committee government: Congress in its committee rooms is Congress at work.'

Examiner tip
Unlike in the UK Parliament, the legislative process in Congress is a very negative process where legislation is particularly difficult to pass. Be aware of all the potential veto points during the process. More importantly, be able to analyse *why* many bills fail to pass or are so heavily amended as to be unrecognisable.

Knowledge check 18

Explain the importance of the congressional oversight process.

Why are the congressional committees so powerful?

- Congressional committees have a key role in the legislative process, reviewing all bills in their area, with power to pigeon-hole, amend or block.
- Their permanence and huge committee staffs mean that they develop policy specialisation and expertise, which balances that of the executive branch.
- They conduct public hearings and have extensive oversight powers over cabinet secretaries or agency heads, with power to subpoena witnesses.
- They have close links with the federal departments and agencies that they oversee and finance, and also with pressure groups. These links are called '**iron triangles**' and can dominate areas of policy making. An example would be the relationships between the 'military-industrial complex' of the Pentagon, the armed services committees and defence contractors.
- The 'blue ribbon' committees are especially important. Examples include those dealing with taxation (Ways and Means) and spending (Appropriations or Senate Finance) and those with influence in foreign policy, such as Senate Foreign Relations. The Judiciary Committee conducts confirmation hearings for Supreme Court justices. The House Rules Committee can block legislation.

Knowledge check 19

Which congressional committees are the most important and why?

Examiner tip

Do not underestimate the importance of congressional oversight as a key function of Congress and the reasons for the powerful role of the congressional committees and their chairs, making sure you have examples of specific oversight activities and impact.

How is membership of congressional committees decided?

Members of committees are chosen by the party committees, and membership is according to party strength. The chairs of the committees are very powerful and always come from the majority party. Most members of Congress want committee assignments affecting their constituency interests, where they can effectively pork barrel. Representatives from farming districts and states will want to be on the Agriculture Committee, while those representing urban districts will want to be a member of a committee dealing with urban affairs. Members 'claim credit' for their committee activities in their re-election campaigns (which their challengers cannot do).

How important is the role of party in Congress?

Congress has a relatively weak party system within it, and members of Congress are relatively independent of strong party ties, but the key word here is 'relatively'.

One reason for the relative lack of party influence is the way that members of Congress are elected. Although all are elected with a party label (apart from a few Independents such as Bernie Sanders from Vermont), they will generally raise their own campaign finance. They also run their own personalised election campaigns based on their individual views and the views prevalent in their districts or states. They have been described as 'independent political entrepreneurs' for this reason. When they have achieved success through their own personal efforts they do not feel beholden to their party for their election. As a result, until recently there has been relatively little party cohesion, with each House member and senator more attuned to their voters' wishes than to their party ties. A good piece of advice to new members of Congress could be 'damn your party and stick to your district'.

Knowledge check 20

What is meant by describing members of Congress as 'independent political entrepreneurs'?

Many members of Congress do have their own ideological views on issues, whether liberal, conservative or moderate, and belong to factions such as the Blue Dog Democrats or the Republican Main Street Partnership, and this influences the way they vote in roll-call votes. But this does not necessarily (or always) coincide with voting with their party.

The USA used to have no equivalent of manifestos or clear mandates, and this perhaps hampered the development of the sort of party cohesion found in the UK. In the 1994 mid-term elections, however, House Republicans ran on a de facto manifesto called the 'Contract with America', containing a clear reform agenda of conservative policies such as a balanced budget that they were all committed to support. Partly in response to this, in 2006 the Democrats ran on a platform called 'Six for 06' outlining six broad legislative goals such as healthcare reform.

Finally, there is some degree of party linkage found in both houses, with the majority of Republicans voting against a majority of Democrats on most issues.

Party influence

Apart from the leadership role in Congress of the committee chairs, there are also majority- and minority-party leaders in both houses who organise party business. There is also the house speaker who is, in effect, a leader of the party caucus and the link between the power centres in Congress. They all serve to provide some degree of party unity and organisation, which is increasing, although not to the levels found in the UK Parliament.

There are also whips, who try to achieve party cohesion in votes through persuasion and bargaining. However, they are limited in their efforts, as there are no carrots of office that can be used to influence members' behaviour and no sticks of discipline to use against rebels voting against their party. However, there is some evidence of attempts to influence party voting, such as increasing party control through allocation of committee assignments.

To some extent, legislative success depends on the persuasion skills of the party power brokers, for example the famous 'Johnson treatment' applied by LBJ to fellow senators when he was Senate majority leader in the 1950s. Success can also depend on the variable persuasion skills of the White House incumbent on different issues at different times. G. W. Bush had support from a House Republican majority in passing his legislative agenda between 2001 and 2006, although Obama struggled to pass his agenda after 2009 without making huge compromises such as those on healthcare reform.

In effect, there is little that can be done to persuade members to vote with their party if they do not wish to. Most votes are bipartisan and there are 'shifting coalitions' of votes on different issues. For example, eight moderate Republican senators, including Susan Collins from Maine and Mark Kirk from Illinois (Obama's home state), voted with the Democrats in 2010 to repeal the Don't Ask Don't Tell policy, which had previously banned active gays from serving in the armed forces.

However, although lacking the party loyalty, discipline and leadership of the UK House of Commons with clear party manifestos and mandates, party membership still provides the best predictor of the vote in both houses of Congress.

Examiner tip

There is evidence of increasing partisanship in Congress. Specific evidence should be found (perhaps from *Congressional Quarterly*) of party voting on issues such as healthcare reform and the stimulus proposals under Obama to demonstrate more partisan voting and more ideologically polarised parties.

Knowledge check 21

Explain why party organisation is relatively weak in Congress.

Growing party cohesion/partisanship in Congress

There is strong evidence of growing party cohesion as a result of the more ideological politics of the Reagan era and its legacy of more coherent ideological conservatism. Since the capture of the House in 2010 under the influence of the Tea Party, the Republican Party in Congress has become more conservative and been very cohesive in voting against the Obama agenda, especially on tax cuts and spending and reducing the deficit.

The Democratic Party also became ideologically more liberal and cohesive, helped by the loss of its southern, conservative wing through electoral defeats or by defections in Congress. This led to more party voting and party unity on votes, but nowhere near the level seen in the House of Commons. There is some evidence that the Democratic Party has become more ideologically cohesive and liberal under the influence of Nancy Pelosi in the House and Harry Reid in the Senate.

Some members of Congress will vote with their party over 90% of the time, others much less so. In general, members of Congress will vote with their party unless there are significant local pressures on them not to do so. Otherwise, the folks back home in the district or state are the most important influence on roll-call votes, which are recorded and can be published back in the district or used by pressure groups.

Pressure groups

Pressure groups and their lobbyists seek access to members of Congress and become active on all issues affecting their interests: for example, the NRA (National Rifle Association) on gun law reform, or the AARP (American Association of Retired People) on Medicare or prescription drug charges. They can gain access and influence by helping to fund campaigns, or providing specialised advice to congressional committees, or because they are representing millions of voters who members of Congress do not want to alienate. Members of Congress also wish to avoid being targeted for electoral defeat if they speak out against powerful lobbies in the USA.

The White House

Do not forget the influence of the White House and the president's congressional liaison team. Presidential persuasion may be effective or not. There may be helpful party linkages; for example, President Obama had Democrat majorities in both the Senate and the House between 2009 and 2011 and he is an ex-senator and therefore a Washington insider, used to the ways of Congress. President Bush, an ex-governor, struggled in his last two lame-duck years to get any agreement from Congress for his political agenda, as did Obama after the Republican takeover of the House in 2011.

The congressional caucuses

These are cross-party coalitions of members of Congress who share the same or similar ideology, ethnicity or regional interests. Examples are the black caucus (all Democrat), who vote and act together on issues relating to the specific interests of black Americans, such as affirmative action, and the Hispanic caucus uniting on issues such as immigration policy. There has been a Tea Party caucus in the House and Senate since 2009.

Knowledge check 22

Explain the increase in partisanship in the Congress, especially since the 1990s.

Knowledge check 23

Apart from party ties, what other factors influence the voting behaviour of members of Congress?

Congress and representation

In addition to its legislative and oversight functions, Congress is the representative assembly for the USA. Both houses of Congress have a function of representation of the views and interests of the people in their districts and states. This is given the highest priority by members of Congress, who take their role as 'representatives of the people' more seriously than most other democratically elected representatives.

Congressional elections

These take place every 2 years, when all the Representatives and one-third of the Senate are elected. The elections tend to be fought around local issues rather than national ones, and there is a 'locality rule' that those standing for election should be residents of the state or district they represent, thus strengthening the idea that 'all politics is local'.

In elections, members of Congress stress their commitment to constituency service rather than loyalty to party, usually leading to a very high re-election rate (over 90%). It is argued that the incumbency advantage is now so great that congressional elections are no longer competitive in very 'safe' districts and states, although members may now be more likely to face primary challenges as some Republicans did in 2010 from Tea Party challengers to their right.

Why are incumbents re-elected?

Incumbency re-election rates are consistently high at over 90%. There are a number of reasons for this:
- their huge resources, such as staffs in the state or district as well as Washington and free mailing for publicity called the 'franking privilege'
- their name and face recognition and 'visibility' in the district or state, thanks to constant local media coverage
- their opportunities to serve their constituents' interests, such as 'bringing home the bacon' to their districts or states and then 'credit-claiming' for all they have done for their constituents while in Washington
- their huge campaign war chests from special interests and political action committees who wish to gain access to them. In the 2012 congressional elections, Senate incumbents raised an average of over $4.6 million each, while the average challenger could only muster around $320,000.
- the gerrymandering of districts by partisan state legislatures redrawing boundaries to make them even more 'safe'. It is worth noting though that hostile re-districting by the other party can pose a significant threat to an incumbent.
- the difficulties faced by any challengers of showing that they could provide a better service to constituents

However, it is still possible for challengers to beat incumbents with, for example:
- an anti-Washington 'kick the bums out' mood in the country, as in 2008 and 2010 when Tea Party influence was evident in many districts and states
- a particularly unpopular member of Congress targeted for defeat, usually because of some ethics scandal. In 2008 for instance, William Jefferson from a very safe

Democrat district in Louisiana failed to be re-elected following allegations of racketeering and bribery. The FBI apparently found $90,000 stashed in one of his freezers.
- a huge campaign war chest to outspend the incumbent. In 2012, for example, Democrat challenger Elizabeth Warren outspent and defeated the Republican incumbent Scott Brown in the Massachusetts Senate race.

But these circumstances have been rare, and only 'open' seats have provided real competition. It is paradoxical that Congress as an institution is highly unpopular in the USA (its approval ratings shrank to an all-time low of 10% according to a poll in September 2013) but most Americans support and vote for their incumbent representative or senator.

Members of Congress and constituency service

The first Congress established that representatives should act as trustees for the whole nation, not as mere delegates of their constituents.

Today, however, the majority of members of Congress spend time on constituency rather than national service, through their successful pork barrelling, which pleases their constituents but does little to reduce budget deficits or the national debt. Members of Congress are the link between their constituents and the huge and impersonal bureaucracies based in Washington, and they help their constituents with problems such as Medicare, veterans' programmes and tax or employment issues. It is these 'home-style' activities that members of Congress can claim credit for that normally secures their re-election.

Criticisms are made of members of Congress who appear too concerned with providing benefits to their home state or district, to the detriment of the national interest of the USA as a whole. However, when they get pork-barrel federally funded projects for their districts, they *are* representing their constituents, just as they are when they oppose progressive income taxes if they represent a wealthy district, or when they support them if they represent a poorer one. No one expects a black congresswoman representing a poor New York district to support agricultural subsidies for Montana wheat growers, but she would be expected to support extended welfare services for her district. Similarly, if funding for space or weapons programmes brings federal jobs to the home state, then the senator should vote for them. Re-election is the true test of democracy, as this is the major check that voters have over their representatives and their behaviour in Congress.

Who should a representative represent?

The key debate is to what extent elected representatives represent:
- their state or district (local interests)
- the party label they were elected on (the party interest)
- the national interest

In reality, elected representatives have to balance all three, often competing pressures, as best they can.

One theory of representation was put forward by Edmund Burke, writing in the UK in the 1770s, who stated that elected representatives are *trustees* of their constituents and the nation. The Burkeian notion is that representatives are elected to exercise their judgement on behalf of those they represent, and they are not merely delegates of their constituents, mandated to speak for their interests alone. There is more to representative democracy than serving the immediate whims of volatile constituents who have very different views on issues anyway; representatives of the people should speak and vote for the good of the whole nation. According to Burke, a Congress full of representatives concerned with narrow constituency interests is not doing what a representative assembly should be doing.

This, however, is increasingly difficult as many legislators, especially in the House, are worried about upsetting the 'core' in their area who are the most likely to vote in a party primary, and may work to defeat a representative they feel is not sufficiently in tune with their own views. The problem is that their views are often more extreme than those of the ordinary voter. So a legislator must also be wary of alienating more moderate and independent voters. They must also of course, as mentioned above, be aware of the national interest and their wider responsibilities.

How representative are members of Congress?

In common with other representative bodies in western democracies, elected representatives in Congress do not accurately reflect the social make-up of America. Despite the huge social, economic, ethnic, racial and religious diversity of the American people, Congress does not 'look like them'. This does not fit with the *resemblance model* of representation, as Congress is largely 'white, male, middle class and middle aged' and dominated by lawyers and other educated professionals. It is worth noting the statistics below following elections to the 113th Congress elected in 2012, which was heralded as the most diverse yet:

- A record number of women were elected. Yet still only 20% of the Senate are female and just 10% of the House.
- Just 10% of the House and 1% of the Senate are African-Americans who comprise roughly 12.5% of the overall population.
- Only 32 members of Congress (out of 535) were from a Hispanic background, while Hispanics comprise around 16% of the US population.
- The first openly gay senator (Tammy Baldwin from Wisconsin) was elected.
- The new Congress is more religiously diverse including the first Buddhist senator, and the first Hindu congressman. It also includes the first openly atheist member (though around 20% of Americans now describe themselves as non-religious).
- Around 40% of Congress are millionaires, and the net worth of all its members is over $2 billion.
- The average age in the House is 58, and in the Senate it is 61. The median age in the USA as a whole is just under 38.

Examiner tip

Understand the key debate in representative theory over the nature of representation and who or what a representative should represent — the 'public interest', using 'judgement' as to what is in the best interest of the whole nation; or the interests of the constituents in the state or district that he or she represents. These are known as the trustee/delegate models.

Knowledge check 25

What is the resemblance model of representation?

Knowledge check 26

How representative socially of the USA is Congress? Why is Congress becoming more diverse (albeit slowly)?

That said, anyone can, in theory, stand for Congress if they fulfil the constitutional age, citizenship and residence requirements. There are no formal barriers to a more socially representative Congress. Despite the figures stated above, it is more diverse now than in the past, with more women and ethnic minority members. This is due to factors such as:

- the changing role of women generally and the growth of political action committees (PACs) supporting women candidates, such as Emily's List
- growing black and Hispanic activism and political involvement
- the impact of majority–minority districts (districts with a black or Hispanic majority) shaped to gain greater representation for minority populations. Following re-districting after the 2010 census, there were 27 districts with an African-American majority and 30 with a Hispanic majority.
- shifting social and religious attitudes

Why is Congress still socially unrepresentative?

- 'Ordinary people' or women, young or minority candidates do not seem to want to be representatives and are reluctant to put themselves forward even if they did.
- The perceived need for high levels of education and skills for a political career acts as a disincentive, as does the adversarial nature of politics as portrayed in the media.
- The need for large campaign war chests excludes those who are not millionaires or those without access to the money needed to run.
- There is a perception that politics is an occupation for rich, white males or for political dynasties such as the Kennedys, Bushes and Clintons.

Examiner tip
Have knowledge of the debate over the nature of social representation and the social, gender, ethnic and age composition of the US Congress.

However, questions arise as to whether a legislature has to be socially representative as well as politically representative. Do you have to be a woman to speak and vote on women's issues? How socially representative does it have to be? Does it really matter that legislatures are not socially representative? How could a legislature be made to be more socially representative and a social microcosm of the nation?

Comparisons with the bicameral Westminster Parliament

- The UK has a parliamentary system of government operating under an uncodified constitution and with no separate elections for the executive and legislature.
- There is a fusion of executive and legislative powers, and the prime minister and cabinet are drawn from the majority party in parliament. As a result, there are fewer effective challenges to the dominant power of the executive.
- The government is responsible to Parliament, and the Commons can remove the executive through a successful vote of no confidence, as in 1979.
- The House of Lords is unelected, with life peers, Church of England bishops, some hereditary peers and until recently the Law Lords. It cannot be defended democratically, but it has successfully challenged the government in many policy areas, and is often regarded as a better protector of civil liberties than the more party- and government-dominated lower chamber.

Summary

After studying this topic you should be able to:

- Explain the powerful constitutional role of the US Congress and its enumerated and implied powers in Article 1.
- Understand the constraints on the power of Congress through the constitutional separation of powers and checks and balances.
- Explain bicameralism and the differences between the election, representation, terms of office, role and powers of the House and the Senate as well as their shared concurrent powers.
- Know the legislative process in Congress and explain why the process is so negative because of numerous veto points and why legislation is more likely to fail than pass, other than in exceptional circumstances.
- Understand the processes of congressional oversight over the executive branch, including the key role of the congressional committees.
- Evaluate the importance of the role of party in Congress, giving reasons for its relative weakness in influencing congressional voting.

- Identify and explain other influences on congressional voting, such as district/state influence, pressure group or ideological influences.
- Explain how and why the role of party has grown in Congress, and how partisanship and ideological cohesion have increased compared to the more bipartisan past.
- Evaluate the importance of the incumbency factor when explaining high re-election rates for sitting members of Congress.
- Know of key debates concerning the nature of democratic representation and whether members of Congress should act as 'trustees' or 'delegates' of their constituents.
- Be able to assess how socially representative recent Congresses have been, and evaluate whether they should or how they could become more socially representative of their constituents.
- Make relevant and appropriate references to the UK Parliament to demonstrate similarity or difference to illustrate understanding.

The executive branch of government

The executive is the core of government, where policy is formed and executed. In the USA there is a **presidential executive**, providing the political leadership of the country. Article 2 of the constitution sets out:

- the popular election of the president through the medium of the Electoral College with a fixed term of 4 years
- the only possible removal of the president by a successful impeachment and trial by the House and Senate
- the specific constitutional powers of the president
- the restriction of the president to two terms of office in the 22nd Amendment

It is the formal separation of powers and resulting checks and balances that distinguish the US presidential system of government from the parliamentary system found in the UK. The political scientist Neustadt argued that, in the 'separated system of shared powers', the power of the president becomes only the 'power to persuade', which includes bargaining and compromise with the legislative branch of government to reach consensus.

presidential executive
In Article 2 all executive power is vested in one president, elected separately from Congress with his own mandate. It is a single-person executive and the president's cabinet (unlike 'cabinet government' in the UK, which is a plural executive drawn from Parliament) has no constitutionally derived power or electoral mandate, and the president may or may not seek their advice when making decisions.

He also argued that the office of president was one of inherent weakness rather than strength, and that the powers of the president were no guarantee that power could actually be exercised. As Lyndon B. Johnson (LBJ) once reportedly said: 'The only real power I have is nuclear and I can't use that.' It is argued that real presidential leadership is possible only in extraordinary crisis conditions such as depression or war. F. D. Roosevelt is often given as the best example of such a president.

The US president is usually but inaccurately seen as the most powerful person in the world. In reality, the constitution restricts the use of executive power, especially in domestic policy, by several means.

The paradox of the US presidency is that despite the apparent omnipotence of the office, with huge expectations of it, there is much evidence of political weakness and many presidencies are characterised by disappointments and failure. This is expressed in terms such as the **imperial presidency** and the **imperilled presidency**, used at different times and under different conditions.

The American presidency is a complex office, with presidents needing many political skills to exercise the constitutional powers granted to them. To some extent the study of the presidency is a study of the person holding the office, the individual's abilities and style, and the circumstances and events surrounding that particular presidency, as well as the office itself. To paraphrase the UK Prime Minister Asquith: 'The office of president is whatever the holder is able, or chooses, to make of it.' One of the enduring debates in US government is 'How powerful is the president?' As in other political debates, the usual answer is 'it depends'. Understanding context is therefore crucial.

What are the constitutional powers of the American president?

The Founding Fathers feared tyranny and an 'elective monarch' above all else, but they were ambivalent about the office of president. They gave the office powers, but also checked these powers, making executive power hard to wield. However, the statement 'all executive power shall be vested in a president of the United States of America' in Article 2 is particularly vague and has led to the stretching of the powers of the office by modern 'activist' presidents in particular, allowing flexibility in their exercise.

Formal, enumerated powers

The president's formal, *enumerated* constitutional powers are as follows:

- **Chief executive.** Executive power is given *only* to the president. The executive branch of government and its coordination are under the president's control and he is responsible for the federal budget, setting out and implementing the policy agenda for the USA. Executive powers also include the powers of patronage and pardon.
- **Commander-in-chief.** The president is leader of the US armed forces and responsible for their deployment.
- **Chief diplomat.** The constitution gives the president the power to make treaties with other countries, although increasingly presidents use 'executive agreements', thus avoiding the need for Senate ratification.

However, these formal constitutional powers are checked and balanced by the independent powers granted to Congress in Article 1 of the constitution.

How have presidential roles developed since the constitution was written?

The office of president today is very different from that envisaged by the framers of the constitution in 1787 — the circumstances that have given rise to modern presidential power could not have been foreseen.

Implied roles and powers

The modern presidency has developed new *implied* roles and powers that are not specified in the codified constitution:

- **Chief legislator.** Although the president has no formal legislative power, most legislation is initiated in the executive branch and presented to Congress in the annual State of the Union Address. The president is not guaranteed to see his legislative proposals enacted into law, but he does have the constitutional power of the regular veto and can exercise a pocket veto at the end of a congressional session. Use of the veto, however, is usually a sign of presidential weakness as it demonstrates that he has failed to persuade Congress to pass legislative proposals in the way he wants. It is often seen as an admission of the failure to persuade.
- **World leader.** The president has huge international status and 'treads the world stage'. This has been particularly the case since the Cold War, the 'war on terror' and the dominance of foreign policy in any presidential agenda.
- **Party leader.** Although not elected as a party leader in the UK sense, the president is seen as a partisan figure. However, as Clinton found out with the defeat of his healthcare proposals in 1994, and Obama with his failure to win the support of all Democrats for gun control measures, he cannot command or even rely on the support of his party in Congress.
- **Head of state.** The president is the only national symbol and the focal point for loyalty. As well as being a political leader, he performs the kind of ceremonial and symbolic functions performed by the queen in the UK as head of state, in effect combining the two roles.

Two factors in particular have allowed the stretching of the power of the office:
- The presidency is the only institution of US government capable of acting quickly and decisively in a crisis such as a terrorist attack, so providing leadership for the country that cannot be provided by Congress.
- The president is the only nationally elected politician speaking for the national interest within a highly fragmented system of government.

However, the balance of power between the president and Congress is not fixed but fluid, and changes with circumstances and events. The ebbs and flows tend to be characterised by a pattern of:
- presidential dominance during times of economic or foreign policy crisis, such as during the Cold War, the great depression or after 9/11
- congressional reassertion of its power when the crisis is over

regular veto The president's constitutional power over legislation he disapproves of, and such a powerful weapon that the threat of a veto can be enough to alter congressional behaviour, risking the successful passage of necessary federal law. It may mean the president fails to get the legislation he desires, as he has failed to persuade and must veto the whole bill, not simply those parts with which he disagrees.

Examiner tip
Always distinguish between the formal powers of the president outlined in Article 2 and those that have developed through custom and practice since the constitution was written (vaguely in the case of presidential power) and that have stretched the power of the office.

Knowledge check 28
What main factors tend to lead to the assertion of presidential power within the system of separated power and associated checks and balances?

Knowledge check 29

Apart from death or
electoral defeat, how can
a president be removed
from office?

The presidency since the 1930s

The power of the modern presidency developed from the 1930s as a result of the growth of federal government intervention in the economy in response to economic depression. It further developed when America moved from an isolationist foreign policy to become the 'world's policeman' after the Second World War, which saw the growth of America's enormous military power and influence in the world. Foreign policy is now largely presidential territory and Congress has generally deferred to the White House in this area, as the nation rallies round the president during conflicts.

The Nixon presidency (1968–72 and 1972–74) was seen as the culmination of the growth of presidential power. The historian Schlesinger in 1973 called this the 'imperial presidency'. Presidential power, however, contained the possibility of the abuse of this power, and this was seen in presidential actions during the Vietnam War and executive abuses of power in the Watergate scandal.

The Congress, both during the Nixon presidency and after Watergate, reasserted its constitutional powers to become the 'resurgent Congress'. It increased its authority over the executive by:

- Increasing congressional resources to make Congress more effective in oversight, such as the setting up of the Congressional Budget Office.
- Passing the Case Act of 1972, forcing the president to inform Congress of all executive agreements made with other states.
- Allowing the passage of the War Powers Resolution in 1973 (vetoed by Nixon but the veto was overridden), restricting, in theory at least, the president's powers to commit troops into hostilities.
- Passing the Budget and Impoundment Control Act in 1974 to prevent the president from impounding (i.e. not spending) money agreed by Congress.
- Rejecting several Nixon appointees to the Supreme Court and federal judiciary.
- The threat of impeachment, leading to the resignation of the 'imperial' Nixon in 1974.

These factors led to new arguments as to whether the post-Watergate presidency (of Ford and Carter in particular) was now not 'imperial' but rather 'imperilled'. The additional constraints came on top of the traditional and long-standing restraints on the exercise of presidential power, by Congress, the Supreme Court and public opinion and the mass media as outlined below.

Congress

The House and the Senate individually or collectively have the power to:
- defeat the president's legislative proposals in the legislative process
- exercise full oversight over his actions and activities
- refuse to fund any of his proposals (even budgets were rejected in 1989 and 1995 and 2012)
- refuse to confirm his appointments, ratify his treaties or declare war
- override his veto with a two-thirds majority in both houses
- impeach him for 'high crimes and misdemeanors'

The Supreme Court

Using the power of judicial review, the Supreme Court can declare the president's actions unconstitutional, as they did in the case of Nixon's claims of executive privilege over the Watergate tapes and in Truman's seizure of the steel mills during the Korean War. George W. Bush, in *Hamdan* v *Rumsfeld* (2006), saw his detention without trial of 'enemy combatants' ruled unconstitutional.

Public opinion and the mass media

The president needs public and media support to deal with Congress, and needs to win over hearts and minds. However, if the president's approval ratings are low, there will be little he can do against hostile public opinion, which will be reflected in increasingly influential, partisan and aggressive news media. This is often the case in the 'lame-duck period' at the end of the fixed two terms of office when there is no possibility of re-election and members of Congress are fixated on their own chances of being re-elected and not likely to defer to a weakening president.

The president and domestic and foreign policy: 'two presidencies'

All presidents try to keep a high profile in foreign policy. This is because they all face difficulties in enacting domestic policy in areas such as health care or welfare and in economic policy, where there is little political consensus between the parties and the branches of government. Most leave office with little achievement in domestic policy, especially after the first year when they try and pass as much of their domestic agenda as possible, as Obama did with healthcare reform when political conditions were most favourable. As a result, they tend to focus on their foreign policy, commander-in-chief role in order to secure their legacy and reputation when they leave office. In foreign policy, Congress usually defers to the president's wishes and he is given a relatively free rein in pursuing his own agenda. This has been referred to as a **bifurcated presidency** — weak in domestic policy, stronger in foreign.

Achieving legislative and policy goals

How can a president try to achieve his legislative and policy goals, given the 'separated institutions sharing power'? He can do so through a variety of means, with some presidents being more successful than others in these areas:

- by his power of persuasion or successful coalition-building skills
- by effective use of his Congressional Liaison Office in the West Wing
- by inviting to the White House or Camp David important members of Congress whose votes he needs
- by campaigning for the re-election of important members of Congress (if he is popular) or staying away (if unpopular)
- by using the media to appeal, over the head of Congress, to the public to support his proposals, as in Roosevelt's 'fireside chats' or modern television appeals by presidents in a crisis. This is called using the 'bully pulpit' to inspire public support of his actions or proposals.

Examiner tip

The presidential–congressional relationship is vital to evaluate, as it illustrates the constraints facing any president when encountering a Congress with its own mandate and constitutionally defined independent powers, and which may be controlled by a party different from that of the president — part of the 'invitation to struggle' encouraged by the constitution.

Knowledge check 30

Explain the checks and balances that the Supreme Court can impose on the president.

Knowledge check 31

Why do presidents become 'lame ducks'?

Knowledge check 32

Explain, using examples, the term 'bifurcated presidency'.

presidential power to persuade Despite formal constitutional powers, the only real power any president has is the power to persuade Congress, executive departments and the public to accept his policies, actions, treaties and appointments; he cannot command or control them. Hence the success of a president depends on his persuasive skills when bargaining, negotiating and coalition building, which vary between presidents and at different times in their presidencies.

The success of the above methods will depend on several variables:

- Whether the president is in his 'honeymoon' (usually the first 100 days or the first year of office), when presidential power can be exercised more successfully, or in his 'lame-duck' final period of office, when power is ebbing away.
- Whether he is in the first or second term of office. Presidents are nearly always weaker in their second term.
- Whether or not he has clear priorities to place before Congress, leadership vision and a governing strategy.
- Whether his public approval ratings are high or low. Bush's were 26% at the end of his second term but over 90% after 9/11. Obama's were over 70% after his 2008 election but had dropped to around 40% by late 2013. This is often linked to the state of the economy or foreign policy.
- Whether he has long electoral 'coat-tails', and therefore majorities of his own party in both houses of Congress, as Obama did in 2008, or no coat-tails and therefore experiences divided party government as has been the case for Obama after the 2010 mid-terms.
- Whether or not he has a strong mandate. President Obama was elected with 53% of the popular vote in 2008 but, uniquely among postwar presidents, secured a smaller share of the popular vote when re-elected in 2012, thereby weakening his mandate for the second term.
- Whether he is a Washington insider (ex-senator) or outsider (ex-governor) and skilled or unskilled in the ways of Washington.
- Whether or not he has good political and leadership skills in persuasion and coalition building. President Obama for instance, has been criticised on this score. Commentator Chris Matthews noted: 'He never developed a love of politics, of politicians...to sit around and play cards with them, get to know them, their nuances, hooks, triggers, buttons. Get to know them and figure out how you can work with some of them.' By contrast George W. Bush was well known for being genial even with his political opponents. This enabled him for example, to work with arch-liberal Democrat the late Ted Kennedy to pass important education reforms in the No Child Left Behind measure.
- The events and circumstances that dominate his presidency. In times of crisis, as we have seen, both the Congress and the Supreme Court tend to defer to the president as he 'wraps himself in the flag' in a wave of national patriotism. It could be argued that Obama's inability to secure convincing congressional support for air strikes on Syria in the middle of 2013 reflected an absence of any perceived threat to national security or a sense of national crisis. The fact that he felt the need to secure the endorsement of Congress in the first place was perhaps also a reflection of his relatively weak mandate and poll standings.

Examples can be found of all the above variables in the studies of different presidents and presidencies and their relationships with Congress at different times and under differing circumstances and events. All modern presidents have had their fair share of successes and failures in their dealings with Congress. It is best to regard their power as dependent upon circumstances, the standing and popularity of the president, their own people skills and personality, and the composition of Congress.

A new 'imperial presidency'?

The aftermath of 9/11 and the subsequent war on terror, which came to dominate the political agenda, saw more concentration of power in the executive. During the G. W. Bush presidency of 2000–04 and after he was re-elected for a second term as the 'war president', debate arose over whether a new 'imperial presidency' was developing, with the expansion of unchecked presidential authority.

Congress was more docile (and the Supreme Court refrained from entering the political thicket in controversial cases). This was helped by Republican control of Congress from 2000 to 2006, with a more ideologically cohesive, conservative Republican party controlling the committees and the legislative process and deferring to President Bush's wishes and demands concerning national security. This was evidenced in:

- the passage of the Patriot Act, with its controversial authority for a 'security state' through domestic surveillance and wire tapping, widely thought to be unconstitutional as it was against the personal freedoms and privacy protected in the amendments
- Guantánamo Bay and the setting up of military commissions to try 'enemy combatant' cases, ignoring the habeas corpus and due process clauses of the constitution
- the setting up of the Homeland Security Department
- the resolution to go to war with Iraq in 2003 (passed by 296 votes to 133 in the House and by 77 to 23 in the Senate), with the costs of war funded
- the increasing use of executive orders and claims of executive privilege

Bush also added *signing statements* to bills before he signed them into law, showing his disapproval of some parts and indicating how he thought they should be applied. In effect this was a line-item veto in all but name, and it was argued that the president was straying too far into legislative action, which was not part of his constitutional power.

So a swinging of the pendulum back towards executive-branch exercise of power between 2001 and 2006 was accompanied by a weakness in congressional oversight.

However, Republican losses in the 2006 mid-term elections, with Congress now in the control of Democrats who were ready to flex their political muscles, left Bush a lame-duck president for his last 2 years of office. He had also alienated many Republicans with his 'big government conservatism' and growing budget deficits.

President Obama

The election of President Obama in 2008, with strong Democrat majorities in both houses of Congress, changed the situation again. In the midst of a severe economic crisis, the new president, a former lecturer in constitutional law, promised a bipartisan, pragmatic approach to the presidential–congressional relationship and the challenges that engulfed America in 2008.

The new president, a Washington insider, took office with:
- a huge personal mandate
- high approval ratings but also sky-high expectations relating to 'hope' and 'change'
- political and personal charisma and the power to persuade

But he has also faced:

- continuing war in Afghanistan and an increasingly unstable and unpredictable world, seen in the Middle East and the Arab countries
- economic depression, high and rising unemployment and an increasing national debt, together with the downgrading of America's Triple A debt rating
- criticisms from the Republican right for going too far to the left, into socialism and 'class warfare', and from the Democratic left for not going far enough and compromising too much with obstructionist Republicans in Congress on health care, economic stimulus and tax cuts
- the lack of a filibuster-proof Senate of 60 Democrat votes

Losing control of the House following the 2010 mid-terms, his less than emphatic re-election in 2012 and the ongoing problems of the economy all suggest that Obama's second term will be even tougher. By the end of 2013, he had been forced to back down from his intention to launch missile strikes against Syria, and like Clinton in 1995–96, faced a federal shut-down as the House refused to pass his budget.

Presidential resources

The institutions of the modern presidency

Huge resources are needed to carry out the role of the modern presidency in the world's biggest government. All executive power may be vested in one president but the reality today is that of a vast 'institutional presidency' within a vast executive branch of government. With the huge growth of government activity in both domestic and foreign affairs, especially since the 1930s, various institutions have developed to help the president fulfil his constitutional roles and much of what is done in the president's name is done by other people. However, the president is the only elected member (apart from the vice-president) with responsibility for all decisions taken. As Truman said when he was president, 'the buck stops here'.

The role of the vice-president

Although the vice-president 'balances the ticket' in a presidential election, the office of vice-president is traditionally perceived to be lacking significance, with no constitutional role apart from presiding over the Senate and brokering a tied vote. However, the office has changed somewhat in recent years: Dick Cheney was believed to be the power behind the throne in the George W. Bush presidency and the most powerful (and criticised) vice-president in US history, and Joe Biden has been fully involved in major policy initiatives and seeking congressional approval for these. A 'heartbeat away from the presidency', the main constitutional significance of the office is that the vice-president will become president if the incumbent president dies in office.

The presidential cabinet

The US cabinet has no constitutional status and is not mentioned in the constitution other than as a possible body of advisers the president *may* take advice from. The US cabinet operates, therefore, by convention; *all* executive power is vested in the

Knowledge check 34

Explain the reasons for the growth of the 'institutional presidency'.

president. The USA has a singular executive, with no collective decision taking or collective responsibility. This is in contrast to a plural executive, such as the UK's cabinet government.

The cabinet contains the heads of the 15 federal government departments; the director of the Office of Management and Budget and the vice-president also attend. The president does not need to call any cabinet meetings and their use has been variable according to the wishes of the president and the circumstances of the time. Nor does he have to take their advice — he has alternative sources of advice in the Executive Office (see below).

What are the functions of the cabinet?

Cabinet members are responsible to the president for the federal departments that they head. As such they:

- Implement the president's agenda in their specialist area.
- Appear before the powerful congressional committees to represent the president's wishes and plead for funding and support for the president's policies.
- Attend meetings with the president, if and when required, to give advice. Often these are bilateral meetings to advise rather than full cabinet ones to discuss. Why would the secretary of state want or need to know what is going on in the Agriculture Department?
- Assist the president when full cabinet meetings are called to coordinate policy between the various federal departments involved in US government.

How is the cabinet selected?

When presidents win office they select their cabinet secretaries during the transition period between November and January when the 'spoils of office' are distributed. There is no shadow cabinet in the USA and the president cannot select his cabinet from Congress because of the separation of powers. If members of Congress accept a cabinet post they must resign their congressional seats.

Otherwise cabinet members can come from anywhere — academia or business, for example — and the president has a free hand in their selection. Generally, the president-elect will be influenced by the following factors in his choices:

- They will be policy specialists, not generalists (as in the UK), chosen for their expertise and ability to head the specific federal department. They may not be politically experienced but will need some political skills to carry out their role.
- They have to be confirmed by the Senate after hearings.
- The president may wish to construct a cabinet which 'looks like America', providing some ethnic, gender or geographical balance and diversity, or, like Obama, a 'cabinet of rivals' to inspire debate.
- Generally, presidents choose political allies to provide partisan support, but they can be from a different party to the president to demonstrate bipartisanship. Thus following his re-election, Obama chose a Republican ex-senator, Chuck Hagel, as defense secretary.

Knowledge check 35

What is meant by describing the role of the US cabinet as 'institutionalised by usage alone'?

spoils of office A newly elected president, perhaps a Washington outsider, must select people for his administration (there is no cabinet-in-waiting or totally permanent bureaucracy as in the UK). The transition period is when the president-elect selects members of the executive branch from outside Congress. Presidents often reward loyal party and campaign supporters with these 'spoils of office' and may try to achieve a social balance in appointments.

How important is the cabinet to the president?

iron triangles and
clientelism All presidents
face the problem of
close relationships that
develop between federal
agencies that administer
programmes, congressional
committees that fund
and oversee them, and
special interests seeking
to influence them
(hence 'triangle') and the
difficulties of breaking
these relationships (hence
'iron'). Clientelism refers
to the strong relationships
that develop between the
agencies and their 'clients',
weakening congressional
oversight and with the
president powerless
to influence these
relationships.

The power of the cabinet is not fixed and unchanging. It depends on variables such as the personalities involved or the governing style of the president. There may be a relatively inexperienced Washington-outsider president, willing to delegate to strong and experienced cabinet members, as in the case of President George W. Bush with Dick Cheney and Condoleezza Rice, for example, with the president relying on them for policy advice. Or there may be a strong Washington-insider president like Kennedy, who rarely called a cabinet meeting.

There is no set pattern, and evidence can be found from the study of different presidents and the variable use of their cabinets and the circumstances and issues dominating at the time (war or peace, recession or economic boom).

It is often said that presidents do not trust their cabinet secretaries' close links and loyalty to the federal department that they head and its permanent bureaucracy, nor their strong links with congressional committees and special interest lobbies because of their shared interests and close relationships. It is feared that they 'go native' or are captured in the so-called iron triangles, where policies are made and executed to the benefit of all parts of the triangle. Presidents are also aware of clientelism, where close links develop between the agencies and those they are supposed to be regulating (known as 'agency capture'). The presidential policy agenda is lost sight of in the process, with the president unable to exercise control.

This is why presidents turn to their political 'cronies' and advisers in EXOP.

The Executive Office of the President (EXOP)

EXOP is an umbrella term covering the various offices that developed after the observation of the 1937 Brownlow Committee, as the role of the presidency grew, that 'the President needs help'. EXOP has been described as the principal instrument of presidential government and as the president's *personal bureaucracy*. Working under the direct control of the president (unlike the cabinet members who may have divided loyalties), EXOP is used to direct and control the executive branch of government. New parts have been added to EXOP since its creation in 1939, as the domestic and foreign policy demands on the president have increased.

Today EXOP includes the following.

The White House Office (WHO)

Examiner tip
It is possible both to
overestimate and to
underestimate the role of
the US cabinet, as different
presidents use their
cabinets in different ways
and as often or as little
as they please, depending
on issues, personalities
and presidential abilities
involved. Always have
some evidence of
presidents using, or not
using, their cabinets for
advice and guidance.

Often described as the invisible presidency, the WHO is made up of the president's closest aides. The key figure is the chief of staff, but the office also includes the president's speechwriters, congressional liaison team and press officers. The function of the WHO is to:
- Act as gatekeeper, controlling access to the president (Nixon's key aides were nicknamed the 'Berlin Wall' for their success in this task).
- Decide policy strategy and priorities for the president.
- Manage the news.
- Build support for the president's proposals in Congress.

The National Security Council (NSC)

Headed by the national security adviser, the NSC advises the president on domestic, foreign and military matters relating to national security. The final decision by Obama to go ahead with the raid that killed Osama bin Laden in May 2011 (Operation Neptune Spear) was made after meetings of the NSC.

The Office of Management and Budget (OMB)

The OMB constructs the federal budget, thus coordinating the legislative priorities and spending plans of the federal government departments and agencies. The OMB may provide different advice to the president from that given by the treasury secretary or the Council of Economic Advisers, which is also in EXOP.

Why is EXOP so important to the president?

The president relies on the advice and expertise of EXOP as an alternative to that coming from the cabinet secretaries, who may have conflicting interests. In contrast, the president trusts his advisers in EXOP, who are loyal only to him and who follow his agenda.

What criticisms are made of EXOP?

- The president can become isolated, remote and overprotected from the realities of life outside the Oval Office, listening only to his 'political cronies', who have often come with him into the West Wing from his home state, and taking advice only from them. Examples include Karl Rove, Bush's close adviser, and David Axelrod for Obama.
- EXOP is unelected and unaccountable despite its huge power and influence, with few of its members subject to Senate confirmation or to congressional oversight as cabinet members are.
- 'Policy drift' occurs, with disputes between the cabinet secretaries and their EXOP counterparts leaving the president perhaps caught between the conflicting advice. Woodward illustrates this in his book *Obama's Wars*, highlighting deep policy disputes between his foreign and security policy advisers on the Iraq and Afghanistan wars.

The role of the federal bureaucracy

The federal bureaucracy consists of the officials in the federal government departments, executive agencies and regulatory commissions, who are employed by the state to advise on and carry out the policies of the political executive, thus exercising bureaucratic power. All these organisations are created and funded by Congress. A bureaucracy is indispensable to the operation of modern government to run the core functions of the state. However, it lacks the legitimacy that comes from election and takes no electoral responsibility for the decisions that are made. It is described as the state's engine room, as it drives everything in government.

In the USA, the 15 federal government departments are headed by cabinet secretaries but staffed by hierarchically organised federal bureaucrats, most of whom are

Knowledge check 36

Why do presidents often rely on their advisors in EXOP for advice and guidance rather than on their cabinet secretaries?

Examiner tip

Remember that any analysis of the presidency and the exercise of presidential power involves much more than simply a study of the president and his constitutional powers, and should always extend into the complex web of relationships within the 'institutional presidency' as well as between the president and the ever-powerful Congress.

bureaucratic power

Bureaucratic power is the power invested in the federal bureaucracy by virtue of the permanence of most officials and their specialised expertise, developed over years of experience in a federal department, agency or commission. In this way, bureaucrats acquire influence over the initiation and implementation of policy. The advice of the permanent bureaucrats is channelled through cabinet secretaries and agency heads, who must answer to Congress for their departments/agencies.

permanent. However, some appointments are political (and therefore temporary) appointments made by an incoming president.

It is argued that permanent status gives bureaucrats detailed policy knowledge and expertise. This, it is argued, allows them to influence policy initiation through their advice on options, and also have control over policy implementation once laws have been passed by Congress and signed by the president. They are therefore in a good position to influence the working of public policy and are accountable only to their political heads, the cabinet secretaries, and, through them, to the president.

In theory, the federal bureaucracy works under the direction of the president, but in practice it is difficult, if not impossible, for a president to 'command and control' and make the bureaucracy do what he wants it to do. As Truman said: 'I thought I was the President but when it comes to these bureaucracies I can't make 'em do a damn thing.' Other presidents have expressed similar sentiments about the relationships between cabinet secretaries, congressional committees, interest groups and federal bureaucrats who have strong views on American public policy and how it should be made and carried out. All presidents, at some stage in their presidency, express reservations about the bureaucracy and their policy views, which become entrenched and hard to change.

Comparisons with the UK executive

The UK executive works under an uncodified constitution, with constitutional conventions largely determining its operation.

The prime minister and cabinet

- Constitutionally, and in theory, the UK has cabinet government with collective decision making and collective responsibility.
- The prime minister is not elected but is simply the majority party leader, who exercises the powers of the royal prerogative.
- Although the prime minister has power over the cabinet, he or she is constitutionally *primus inter pares* — first among equals — within it, and the prime minister's patronage appointments are not checked by the legislature.
- There are arguments that the office has become 'presidentialised', but this may be to do with the personal governing styles of certain 'strong' prime ministers and the growth of prime ministerial resources.

The UK civil service

- The UK civil service is permanent, neutral and selected by merit. There are no political appointments of civil servants or 'spoils of office'.
- The civil service is anonymous. It works under the direction and control of elected ministers.
- It is sometimes argued that a 'rule by officials' lies behind a façade of representation and accountability. The problem of organisation and control of bureaucratic power is one that no political system finds easy to solve.

After studying this topic you should be able to:

- Explain the nature of the US presidential executive and its constitutional role under Article 2.
- Understand the paradoxical nature of presidential power, which can be both 'imperial' and 'imperilled' at different times, with, it is argued, only the 'power of persuasion' to drive forward the presidential agenda.
- Explain the formal, enumerated constitutional powers of the president in Article 2 as chief executive, chief diplomat and commander-in-chief.
- Understand that the president's formal constitutional powers have been stretched as circumstances have changed and other presidential roles have developed.
- Know of the checks and constraints on the exercise of presidential power through constitutionally shared powers and checks and balances, and the independent power of Congress (and the Supreme Court).
- Understand that presidential power can be different according to whether it is exercised in foreign or domestic policy.
- Evaluate the variable factors that may allow the president to achieve his legislative goals and other factors that may hinder the progress of his policy agenda.
- Give examples from modern presidencies of either success or failure in different policy areas and reasons for these.
- Understand that important resources have developed to assist the president in carrying out his role, including the vice-president, the cabinet and the Executive Office of the President (EXOP) in an 'institutional presidency'.
- Know the role of the cabinet and also of EXOP and the criticisms that can arise of both executive bodies.
- Know that the US government is administered by a vast, unelected and permanent federal bureaucracy, which carries out the functions of the state and which, many argue, exercises power through the expertise and advice of its officials, while remaining unaccountable.
- Make relevant and appropriate references to the UK parliamentary executive of prime minister, cabinet and civil service to illustrate similarities or differences.

Summary

The judicial branch of government: the Supreme Court

The judicial power of the Supreme Court, the third branch of US government, comes from Article 3 of the constitution. The Supreme Court was to be the guardian of the sovereign, entrenched document, containing the USA's fundamental law and core values.

The court today plays a very different role from that envisaged in 1787 and debate revolves round whether it can be seen as a political as well as a judicial institution, with the justices simply 'politicians in robes sitting on a bench'.

Why is the Supreme Court so important in the US system of government?

- The Supreme Court has the power of constitutional interpretation of the vague language of the document and its amendments.

constitutional interpretation 'We are under a constitution but the constitution is what we say it is' refers to the Supreme Court's role as the ultimate, authoritative interpreter of the meaning of the words in the constitution and its amendments. These often deliberately vague words require interpretation, particularly as the USA has evolved and changed since 1791. The court has changed its mind several times over the meaning of the words in the document.

- The Supreme Court resolves the conflicts that arise over the constitutional workings of the branches and layers of American government, and over the protection of rights entrenched in the Bill of Rights.
- By convention, the Supreme Court has the power of judicial review, which it 'discovered' in the *Marbury* v *Madison* case of 1803 when it first declared an Act unconstitutional.

What is judicial review?

The power of judicial review allows the Supreme Court to declare laws or parts of laws passed by Congress and the president to be incompatible with the constitution and therefore void. An example would be the use of the line-item veto struck down by the court in *Clinton* v *City of New York* in 1998. The first time the court declared a state law unconstitutional was in the *Fletcher* v *Peck* case in 1810. Presidential actions can also be declared unconstitutional, as, for example, Nixon's claim of executive privilege over the Watergate tapes in 1973.

This power of judicial review was not in the constitution itself. The *Marbury* v *Madison* (1803) judgement effectively determined that the constitution is superior to the laws passed by Congress, thereby increasing the interpretational power of the Supreme Court. The court's power of judicial review over presidential, congressional and state actions, determining their constitutionality, is the main reason why the Supreme Court is often described as a political as well as a judicial institution.

A brief history of the Supreme Court

Until 1865, cases coming before the court involved issues relating to federal–state relations and slavery. For example, the *Dred Scott* v *Sandford* case in 1857 concluded that slavery was constitutional. From the 1870s to the 1940s, cases related more to state regulation of the economy. With economic issues largely settled, the emphasis then shifted to civil liberties and civil rights cases, such as those determined by the Warren and Burger courts in the mid-twentieth century. These were both 'judicially activist' courts, whereas the Rehnquist Court (1986–2005) was a court of more 'judicial restraint'. The current court is the Roberts Court whose approach will be examined on pp. 48–49.

How are Supreme Court justices appointed?

Supreme Court judges are nominated by the president when vacancies occur either through death, such as Rehnquist in 2005 or resignation/retirement, such as Stevens in 2010. Their nomination must, however, be approved by a majority vote in the Senate. There is no guarantee therefore on how many (if any at all) nominations presidents can make during their time in the White House. No vacancies occurred under Carter's presidency, while by the end of his first term as president, Obama had been able to make two nominations — justices Sotomayor and Kagan. The fact that both president and Senate are involved in the appointment process has added to the politicised nature of Supreme Court nominations and confirmation:

- Presidents use their power of nomination to reinforce their political position and to leave a legacy on the Supreme Court. Presidents have a maximum of 8 years in office, whereas their Supreme Court nominee(s) can be on the court for decades. This has led to mention of the Supreme Court being an 'echo chamber' of past presidents.

- Presidents can use their power of nomination to gain support from key groups, for example Lyndon Johnson's appointment in 1967 of the first black justice, Thurgood Marshall, and Reagan's 1981 appointment of the first female justice, Sandra Day O'Connor. Obama's 2009 nomination of Sonia Sotomayor was partially linked to her Hispanic roots and the increasing importance of the Hispanic vote.
- Republican presidents nominate 'conservative' justices with a philosophy of judicial restraint and 'strict constructionism'. Democrat presidents nominate 'liberal' justices with a philosophy of judicial activism and 'loose constructionism'. (These terms are covered in more detail below under 'Judicial philosophy'.)
- The appointment process is particularly important when 'swing' justices retire or die and have to be replaced. Their departure may alter the balance of the Supreme Court thus affecting the judgements likely to be made. This was the case when 'swing' Justice Sandra Day O'Connor retired and was replaced by the more judicially conservative Samuel Alito in 2006. The current 'swing' justice is Anthony Kennedy.
- Presidents also have to ensure that their nominees are likely to get through the Senate vote. Relevant judicial expertise is therefore necessary, as well as the nominee not being perceived as being too extreme or controversial. This has not always, however, been the case.

Several judicial appointments have been particularly controversial:

- In 1987, the Senate rejected Reagan's nominee, Robert Bork. Although a distinguished legal scholar, Bork's highly conservative judicial views were unacceptable to the Democrat-controlled Senate. By rejecting the nomination, the Senate denied Reagan his wish to shift the court towards a more conservative judicial philosophy.
- George Bush's nominee in 1991, the black but highly conservative Clarence Thomas, scraped through the Senate Judiciary Committee hearings after the lowest American Bar Association rating ever for a potential justice and was only just confirmed by the whole Senate on a vote of 52 to 48.
- G. W. Bush's initial nomination of his White House counsel, Harriet Miers, to replace Rehnquist in 2005 had to be withdrawn after it became clear that her lack of judicial experience meant confirmation was unlikely, even from a Republican-controlled Senate.

There is strong evidence that Senate confirmation votes are becoming increasingly partisan. For instance, back in 1993 Ruth Ginsburg was confirmed by 96–3 votes, while in 2010 another nominee, Elena Kagan, from a Democrat president, was only approved by 63–37 votes when 36 out of 41 Republican senators voted against her nomination. This is perhaps a recognition of the political importance of many of the court's judgements as well as a sign of the increased partisanship in Congress.

The importance of the president's powers of appointment can, however, be over-estimated:

- As mentioned above, the president can appoint only when a vacancy arises, i.e. when a justice has died or retired. Some presidents are fortunate and get to appoint several justices, others, such as Carter, do not get to appoint any.
- The president cannot remove justices or influence their judgements once they are on the court.
- He has no guarantees that justices will do what he wants, as their future decisions are unpredictable. Some presidents express regrets about their choices; Eisenhower

Knowledge check 38

What are 'swing' justices, and why are they important?

Examiner tip

The two-stage process for the selection of Supreme Court justices is described as highly politicised. You must be able to explain the political factors involved in *both* presidential nomination *and* Senate confirmation, giving reasons, with examples, why presidents nominate certain kinds of justice, and why their confirmation may be politically controversial.

Examiner tip

Always be aware that the 'politicised' nomination power can be exaggerated. Stress its limitations for accurately predicting what will happen in the future and be able to give evidence to demonstrate the fact that, once on the court, justices cannot be influenced or controlled.

Knowledge check 39

Explain the importance of the independence of the judiciary in the US political system.

loose constructionism Loose constructionist justices, such as Ruth Bader Ginsburg, usually appointed by Democratic presidents, interpret the 'living constitution' flexibly, reading things into it in a 'loose' or 'liberal' way. They reject ideas of 'original intent', arguing that it is impossible to establish what the framers intended, as they are not here and could not have foreseen the changes that would come about. Conservative critics call this 'legislating from the bench' and judicial arrogance.

judicial activism An activist court asserts its judicial power and sees the role of the court as bringing about desired social outcomes such as equality and justice, changing society for the better, and not waiting for action from the elected branches or deferring to their electoral mandates. It means adapting the constitution through interpretation to fit changing social conditions with reference to contemporary social needs and values, such as racial and gender rights.

referred to his selection of fellow conservative Earl Warren as chief justice as 'the biggest damn fool mistake I ever made' when Warren went on to lead the most activist court in US history. More recently, George Bush senior nominated David Souter in 1990, only for him to become one of the most liberal leaning justices in the court by the time he retired in 2009.

- The current Supreme Court has five Republican-nominated justices and four Democrat ones, but it is not a reliably predictable court (see pp. 48–49).

Judicial independence

This is the principle that there should be a strict separation between the judiciary and the other branches of government, and is fundamental to the idea of the rule of law. Judges operate free from any political control over their behaviour. The key to judicial independence is security of tenure, with judges holding office for life, on condition of 'good behaviour'. They cannot be removed for political reasons or for the judgements they make; they can be removed only through successful impeachment by the House and Senate for reasons of personal conduct. The only Supreme Court judge to be impeached was Samuel Chase back in 1805.

Judicial philosophy

To understand the Supreme Court it is important to be aware of different judicial philosophies leading to different views on the interpretation of the constitution by justices. Courts can be judicially active or judicially restrained, depending on the use of their power of judicial review. The Warren and Burger courts, as mentioned above, were judicially activist. The Rehnquist Court was more judicially restrained. The verdict is still out on the Roberts Court. Some of its most prominent cases are listed below, so you might want to make up your own mind by considering its record thus far.

What is judicial activism?

Judicially active justices and courts are those that adhere to loose constructionism. This means that they interpret the words of the constitution in the light of modern conditions and current reality, reading into the words of the constitution their views of what is best for the country at the present time, linking to ideas of a 'living constitution' changing over time without formal amendment.

A judicially active court of loose construction, such as the Warren Court, would use the power of judicial review to 'innovate' through landmark rulings: for example, extending civil liberties and rights and generally favouring the expansion of federal power.

The Warren Court 1953–69 and the Burger Court 1969–86

The Warren Court took the initiative in several areas where the elected branches of government, president and Congress, were either unable or unwilling to act. The court had a huge impact on American life through many of its judicial decisions, in particular the following:

- *Brown* v *Board of Education of Topeka, Kansas* (1954). The court ruled (9–0) that the 'separate but equal' doctrine established in the *Plessy* v *Ferguson* case in 1896 was unconstitutional and inherently unequal as it denied the 'equal protection of the laws' clause of the 14th Amendment. This case began the dismantling of racial segregation in the USA and galvanised the Civil Rights Movement.

- *Miranda* v *Arizona* (1966). This judgement led to 'Miranda rights', based on the 5th Amendment, requiring the police to remind arrested suspects of their rights including that of remaining silent, and that any answers they give may be used against them in court.

The judgements of the Warren Court became a factor in the 1968 presidential election, when Nixon pledged to put on to the court 'law and order' judges who would 'interpret the Constitution and not impose their own beliefs' or 'legislate from the bench'.

The Burger Court was predicted to be more judicially restrained than the Warren Court but was more activist than expected, and many of its judgements were, and continue to be, controversial:

- *Roe* v *Wade* (1973). Using the shadows or 'penumbras' of the constitution, the court ruled (7–2) that abortion was constitutional and part of a woman's implied right to privacy. This decision, in effect, brought about the 'pro-choice' and 'pro-life' movements that are so active in American political life today. The religious right in particular has lobbied for a constitutional amendment to overturn *Roe* v *Wade*, as the Supreme Court has always upheld its 1973 judgement as established precedent.
- *Swann* v *Charlotte-Mecklenburg Board of Education* (1971). The court made a controversial decision allowing bussing to end 'de facto' segregation and achieve more racial balance in schools under the 'equal protection' clause of the 14th Amendment.

The Warren and Burger courts are good examples of the enormous political and social effects of Supreme Court judgements, as opposed to the decisions made by the president and Congress. Both courts alienated American conservatives and provoked a backlash against what was seen as an 'imperial judiciary' and the quasi-legislative power of the Supreme Court. The question was, and still is, were the justices behaving like politicians, and was the court behaving like a legislature? Regardless of the moral rightness of the justices' decisions and their desirable outcomes, was the court the right institution to take them?

What is judicial restraint?

Judicially restrained justices and courts are those that follow a judicial philosophy of **strict constructionism** and **original intent**. This means that they interpret the constitution more literally and make their judgements based on the words of the original document as written by the Founding Fathers and their intentions at the time. This involves a much narrower interpretation of the constitution. Generally speaking, a court of **judicial restraint** avoids innovation and controversial landmark rulings, favours states' rights and follows precedent (*stare decisis*). It is said that such courts do not wish to enter the political thicket on controversial cases, usually deferring to the elected and responsible branches of government.

The Rehnquist Court 1986–2005

This court, headed by Rehnquist (appointed chief justice by Reagan), was a more restrained court compared to the previous courts. However, it was not easily classifiable and was often divided in its judgements between four 'conservative' justices (Rehnquist, Scalia, Thomas and Kennedy) and four 'liberal' justices (Souter,

Knowledge check 40

Explain the significance of the judgements of the Warren Court.

Knowledge check 41

Why was the 1973 *Roe* v *Wade* case a landmark judgement of the Burger Court?

strict constructionism A strict construction of the constitution's words prevents justices deciding cases on the basis of their own personal values, when they have not been elected to do so, and are not responsible for any outcomes. Strict constructionists deny that rights can be discerned in the constitution's words and argue that the framers could not have had views on abortion or affirmative action, so the court should leave such matters to the elected and responsible branches.

original intent Linked with strict constructionism, 'originalists' like Scalia make judgements on the basis of the 'original intent' of the framers when writing the words of the constitution, closely following the literal text. They believe that constitutional principles are fixed and do not evolve with the times, and that the court should not 'legislate from the bench' like an 'imperial judiciary'.

judicial restraint
This is a more cautious approach to interpreting the constitution, in a 'strict', literal or conservative way, and trying to stay out of 'the political thicket'. A restrained court often stresses the power of the states rather than the federal government. It tends to accept precedent established in past decisions (the principle of *stare decisis*) and defers to the elected and responsible branches, refusing to 'legislate from the bench' and avoiding political controversies.

Knowledge check 42

Explain the controversy surrounding the *Bush* v *Gore* case in 2000.

Breyer, Stevens and Ginsberg). The crucial member of this court was Sandra Day O'Connor, as she was the deciding swing justice on many of the 5–4 knife-edge decisions. A significant 5–4 case, decided in 2000, was *Bush* v *Gore*, which ruled that the Florida recount of ballots after the close election of that year was unconstitutional under the 'equal protection' clause of the 14th Amendment. This case was highly politically charged; in effect, the judgement by the court, seven of whose members had been appointed by Republicans, including two by his father, handed the election to George W. Bush.

The Roberts Court from 2005

The death of Chief Justice Rehnquist and the retirement of Sandra Day O'Connor gave Bush the opportunity to reshape the Supreme Court and leave a conservative legacy on it. He expressed admiration for the two strictest constructionists on the court, Scalia and Thomas, and, in 2005, nominated John Roberts to replace Rehnquist. Roberts was confirmed by a 78–22 vote in the Senate, showing some controversy (Senator Obama voted against the nomination). The court was seen as gaining a conservative boost when the swing justice, Sandra Day O'Connor, retired and was replaced by Samuel Alito, who was widely viewed as a conservative. The two subsequent appointments by Obama of Sotomayor and Kagan have not altered the balance of the Court as both were liberals replacing liberals. The question remains however, how conservative has the Roberts Court been to date. This is best examined by looking at some of the key cases that it has heard.

Cases supporting the argument that the Roberts Court has generally been conservative

- It has been willing to support some limits to abortion, and thus chip away at *Roe* v *Wade*. In *Gonzales* v *Carhart* (2007) a 5–4 majority ruling upheld the constitutionality of the law passed by Congress in 2003 banning partial-birth abortions. This case may be evidence of the difference that a change in justice can bring about (a similar law had previously been struck down).
- It has defended the rights of gun-owners when in June 2008 in *District of Columbia* v *Heller*, it struck down (5–4) a Washington DC gun law banning hand guns as incompatible with the 2nd Amendment. Thus it upheld an *individual's* constitutional right to bear arms. This was the first pronouncement on the 2nd Amendment in the entire history of the Supreme Court.
- It has significantly watered down efforts to regulate campaign finance expenditure. *Citizens United* v *Federal Election Commission* (2010) was a landmark 5–4 decision, with Kennedy joining Scalia, Thomas, Alito and Roberts in the majority to strike down some provisions of the 2002 McCain–Feingold campaign finance legislation as unconstitutional. It overturned earlier rulings such as the 2003 *McConnell* v *FEC* 5–4 decision prohibiting corporate or union involvement in election campaigns through spending from their general funds. The conservative majority now ruled that corporations and unions have the same 1st Amendment free speech rights as individuals in election campaigns, which Justice Stevens in a 90-page dissent called 'a radical change in the law'. This decision was re-affirmed in a 2011 case, *Arizona Free Enterprise Club* v *Bennett*, which struck down an Arizona state law that provided escalating public funds to candidates who accept public funding for their election campaigns.

- It has been seen as too close an ally of corporate rights over and above those of workers and small businesses. In 2011, *Wal-Mart* v *Dukes*, the right of employees to take class action against their employees was weakened. This was strengthened in 2013 with the *American Express Co.* v *Italian Colors Restaurant* case, which made it harder for small companies to take class action suits against large corporations.
- It has also often favoured police powers over the rights of criminals. The ruling in *Maryland* v *King* (2013), for example, upheld the right of the authorities to take and use DNA samples without a specific reason.

Cases opposing the argument that the Roberts Court has generally been conservative

- It has largely upheld the rights of detainees in Guantánamo Bay. One controversial case, decided in 2006, was *Hamdan* v *Rumsfeld*. The court made a landmark that the president had exceeded his constitutional powers as commander-in-chief by setting up military commissions detaining prisoners in Guantánamo Bay. President Bush had argued that this was justified in the war on terror. The court ruled that the 'enemy combatants' (al-Qaida suspects) were entitled to due process of law, thus defending civil liberties in the face of an overpowerful executive and, in effect, reining in an 'imperial presidency'.
- It has upheld the key parts of Obamacare (Patient Protection and Affordable Care Act) in the 2012 *Sibelius* case. Interestingly, in this case it was not the swing justice Kennedy who tipped the balance in a 5–4 case, but Chief Justice Roberts himself.
- It has protected and strengthened gay rights. In a couple of 2013 landmark cases, *United States* v *Windsor* and *Hollingsworth* v *Parry*, in two more 5–4 rulings the court effectively struck down the Defense of Marriage Act and enabled the resumption of same-sex marriage in California.

The protection of rights by the Supreme Court

The 'inalienable rights' of US citizens are entrenched in the first ten amendments, the Bill of Rights, and are protected by the Supreme Court, using its powers of constitutional interpretation and judicial review. It is important to note that the court often has to balance competing rights in its judgements; there are no absolute rights.

Rights of minorities

Grutter v *Bollinger* (2003) said that racial profiling was constitutional for university admissions if it was 'individualised' and not done by quotas or preferential treatment.

Religion

Engel v *Vitale* (1962) upheld the 1st Amendment's guarantee of freedom of religion and denial of an establishment of religion. It was the Founding Fathers' wish for a separation of church and state, so there could be no prayers (or religious activity) in schools or public places.

Freedom of speech

Citizens United v *Federal Election Commission (FEC)* (2010) ruled that corporations and unions have the same 1st Amendment free speech rights as individuals in election campaigns (see above).

Knowledge check 43
How fair is it to describe the Roberts Court as consistently conservative?

entrenched rights
The rights found in the Bill of Rights, the first ten amendments, and rights established in later amendments such as the 14th Amendment's commitment to 'equal protection', are constitutionally protected from easy change by temporary governments and intended to restrict the powers of the federal government (and state governments when the Bill of Rights was extended to the states) over citizens.

Examiner tip
Make sure you can always give examples of important cases from different courts at different times under their chief justice, showing evidence of different judicial philosophies affecting the decisions of the court, especially in important landmark cases. Also watch for any important cases currently before the court.

There are many Supreme Court cases involving the protection of citizens' rights where the ruling is derived from interpretation of the constitutional amendments. There are certainly many more than the oft-quoted 1954 *Brown* and 1973 *Roe* cases. It is important to refer to a range of cases when evaluating the protection (or not) of different kinds of rights by the court.

Knowledge check 44

Why was the *Citizens United* v *Federal Election Commission* Supreme Court judgement controversial?

Knowledge check 45

Why is it difficult to overturn Supreme Court interpretation of the constitution?

Synder v *Phelps* (2011) upheld the 1st Amendment right of the notoriously homophobic Westboro Baptist Church (of God hates fags infamy) to protest outside military funerals.

What are the main constraints on the power of the Supreme Court?

There is little doubt that the Supreme Court's powers of constitutional interpretation and judicial review give it enormous power in the US system of constitutional government and many of its landmark cases have been politically controversial. However, the court is *not* all-powerful and it operates under several constraints. These are as follows:

- It is a reactive court and only rules on cases that are appealed to it and which it agrees to hear. It does not initiate its own cases.
- Congress has power to alter the number of justices on the court. This was threatened when the court was obstructive to parts of the New Deal and Roosevelt threatened his 'court-packing' plan to overcome this obstruction. The court backed down and the numbers on the court have not been changed since the 1869 Judiciary Act.
- Supreme Court interpretation of the constitution can be overturned by constitutional amendment, as in 1913 when the 16th Amendment allowed a federal income tax to be levied, thus overcoming the Supreme Court's ruling that this was unconstitutional. This has been suggested as a way of dealing with issues such as abortion or flag burning, where the court's decisions have angered groups, who then lobby for an amendment. If one were passed, the Supreme Court would have to interpret the new amendment — it could not overturn it. However, although often threatened, this eventuality is unlikely to occur, as it would be difficult to gather the required support in Congress and the states.
- The court can exercise judicial self-restraint by refusing to hear cases appealed to it. An example is the *Schiavo* 'right to die' case in 2005. Decisions to ignore cases indicate that the court is deferring to the elected branches of government and refusing to enter the political thicket or go against prevailing public opinion or established precedent on particular issues.
- The court lacks the power to enforce its decisions as it lacks both the power of the purse and the power of the sword) and has to rely on both political and public acceptance that its decision was the 'right' one. In 1954 the court was unable to enforce its decision in the *Brown* v *Board of Education* case to de-segregate 'with all deliberate speed'. The southern states refused to de-segregate, claiming that states' rights allowed them not to. In 1957 President Eisenhower famously had to send federal troops into Little Rock, Arkansas, to enforce de-segregation of the high school, and, 10 years after *Brown*, the southern states were still not fully de-segregated. The Civil Rights Act finally ended segregation by federal law in 1964.
- Some Supreme Court decisions are ignored, as with the continuation of religious activity in some public areas despite the court's ruling in *Engel* v *Vitale*. Several states have also placed legal restrictions in the way of women seeking abortions.
- It is also worth noting that current courts are not bound by previous rulings. They can and do reverse earlier rulings. Take for example the case of homosexuality. In 1986 the court in *Bowers* v *Hardwick* upheld a Georgia state law that criminalised homosexuality. This was reversed in a later case, *Lawrence* v *Texas* (2003) when

Justice Kennedy went on to write: '*Bowers* was not correct when it was decided, and it is not correct today. It ought not to remain binding precedent.' This is a classic statement showing the temporary nature of many of its decisions, sometimes within a relatively short period of time.

The Supreme Court: a 'political' or 'judicial' body?

This has always been one of the central debates in American government and there are no right or wrong answers to it. Some commentators have used terms such as 'judicial policy making' and 'quasi-legislative judicial authority' to show the contradictions. It is not an easy question to answer because the role of the Supreme Court is paradoxical.

A political body?

On the one hand, these nine persons, appointed for life, meet behind closed doors to make decisions, often with a narrow margin of 5–4, on the major political issues affecting the American people, with no accountability to anyone for those decisions. They will deliberate and make rulings on highly charged and often deeply politicised issues such as:

- Is abortion constitutional?
- Can hand-guns be banned?
- What are the limits on free speech?
- Is gay marriage permissible in the USA?
- Can suspected terrorists be held at Guantánamo Bay without trial?
- Is the death penalty 'cruel and unusual' punishment?

They are also able, through the power of judicial review, to strike down decisions made by the democratically elected representatives of the people in the White House, Congress and the states. It can strike down (and has done so) the results of citizens' initiatives such as Prop 8 in California.

Whereas, in the USA, it is the Supreme Court that decides controversial political questions like those listed above, in other countries, such as the UK, those same issues would be decided by elected and accountable politicians and regarded as political rather than judicial questions. In this sense, the Supreme Court is not and cannot be 'above politics'. Its powers of constitutional interpretation of the codified document and its entrenched rights and of judicial review of state and congressional legislation and presidential actions inevitably bring it into the political arena and give it a political role and some degree of judicial power.

A judicial body?

On the other hand, the Supreme Court is an independent judicial institution and follows judicial procedures. The nine members are justices who believe it their duty to interpret the words of the sovereign constitution in order to ascertain its meaning. They are not politicians representing and accountable to electorates. They have used their powers selectively and sparingly over the 225 years of the court's existence.

Examiner tip
Despite its vitally important role in the American system of constitutional government, be careful not to overestimate the power of the Supreme Court and be prepared to present arguments and evidence of constraints on its power and authority.

Knowledge check 46
What is meant by the phrase 'refusing to enter the political thicket'?

Knowledge check 47
Give examples of changing Supreme Court judgements on the constitutionality of gay rights.

judicial power It may be argued that, since the court is the final arbiter of the meaning of the words in the constitution, this fact, as well as its considerable power of judicial review, places it above both elected branches because all public policies, laws and actions can be challenged as unconstitutional and, if successful, declared void. This is sometimes described as 'government by judiciary' rather than the court being 'the least dangerous branch', as Hamilton claimed.

The central paradox

Finally, it is said that the central paradox of the USA, which takes so much pride in its elective democracy, is the existence of the unelected Supreme Court and its unchecked power to decide crucial questions. The court provides constitutional solutions to what elsewhere would be seen as political problems to be decided politically and not judicially. A final key question, therefore, is 'Who guards the guardians?'

Comparisons with the UK judiciary

Examiner tip
Can the Supreme Court be best described as a political or a judicial body, and are the judges 'nine politicians in robes sitting on a bench'? These are the questions that are asked about the role of the Supreme Court in the US system of constitutional government and the arguments on both sides of the debate should be known.

- In the UK, there is no entrenched codified constitution needing judicial interpretation.
- Parliamentary sovereignty means there can be no challenge to laws passed by parliament.
- The judiciary can only issue 'declarations of incompatibility' if it thinks that parliamentary legislation contravenes the provisions of the 1998 Human Rights Act.
- The judiciary in the UK is therefore less powerful than its counterpart in the USA, with much weaker powers of judicial review.
- Rights are less protected in the UK because they are not entrenched (and cannot be because of parliamentary sovereignty).
- The 2005 Constitutional Reform Act set up an independent Judicial Appointments Commission (JAC) to appoint judges, with no confirmation process in parliament.
- In 2010, the 12 Law Lords moved from the House of Lords to a new 'Supreme Court', strengthening the separation of powers, although they still operate under parliamentary sovereignty.

Summary

After studying this topic you should be able to:
- Identify and explain the role of the Supreme Court as established in Article 3 of the constitution.
- Explain the significance of the power of judicial review, which gives the court such a powerful role in American political life.
- Show the importance of different judicial philosophies which characterise the way in which the court and its individual justices approach judicial decision making, such as activism and restraint, strict and loose constructionism and the doctrine of 'original intent'.
- Give examples of the ways in which different courts have operated and refer to landmark cases made by the Warren, Burger, Rehnquist and Roberts courts and trends in judicial decision making.
- Explain the importance of the protection of entrenched citizens' rights, and refer to key cases where the court has or has not protected those rights.

- Recognise the inevitability of the fact that, whatever the court decides in controversial cases, its decision will alienate one group or another and be criticised by both liberals and conservatives at different times.
- Understand that, despite its constitutional authority, there are constraints on the Supreme Court's power and it has not always gained acceptance or enforcement of its decisions.
- Explain the paradoxical nature of the Supreme Court as a judicial body that makes important judgements with profound political effects.
- Evaluate the arguments as to whether the Supreme Court can best be characterised as a judicial or a political institution, or whether it displays characteristics of both.
- Make relevant and appropriate comparisons with the less powerful UK judiciary, where parliamentary sovereignty prevails.

Questions & Answers

This section looks at answers to examination questions on Unit 4A and follows the four areas previously identified in the specification.

The unit test explained

Unit 4A is 90 minutes in length and you must answer two questions from a choice of four. The questions will reflect the four parts of the unit described earlier.

Each of the four questions has two parts:

- Part (a) is worth 10 marks (maximum 4 for AO1, 4 for AO2 and 2 for AO3) and is a short-answer question. This should be completed in around 8–10 minutes. If you spend more time on this, you will eat into the time needed to complete the essays that are designed to 'stretch and challenge'.
- Part (b) is worth 30 marks (maximum 12 for AO1, 12 for AO2 and 6 for AO3) and is an extended essay. At least 30–35 minutes should be spent on each of the two essays chosen.

Assessment objectives at A2

Although the three assessment objectives at A2 are the same as at AS, they are weighted differently. At A2 more marks are awarded for analysis (AO2) than for knowledge (AO1). The assessment objectives are as follows:

- **AO1:** Demonstrate *knowledge* and *understanding* of relevant institutions, processes, political concepts, theories and debates.
- **AO2:** *Analyse* and *evaluate* political information, arguments and explanations, and identify parallels, connections, similarities and differences between aspects of the political systems studied.
- **AO3:** *Construct* and *communicate* coherent arguments, making use of a range of appropriate political vocabulary. Here the weighting of 20% is the same at AS and A2.

When you write your answer both to part (a) and part (b), you will be given marks for all three of these assessment objectives. These will be totalled to give the mark for each part of the question, with a maximum score of 40 (10 + 30) for each question. This means that the total mark can be achieved in a variety of ways, and students may show different strengths or weaknesses in their answers. Generally, a very good student will achieve high marks on all three assessment objectives. However, it is possible to gain high marks for one objective and lower marks for another. For example, a student's knowledge of a topic may be impressive but the answer may lack clear focus and analysis and it may not be clearly communicated. This means the mark may be high on AO1 but lower on AO2 and AO3. You should be aware of these assessment objectives and practise them throughout the year in homework essays and timed essays in class.

How to achieve good grades

- Make sure you have covered all the specification topics in your revision.
- Consult past papers, mark schemes and assessment objectives to understand how examiners will mark your answers.
- In the examination, answer the question that has been set, not the one you wish had been set. Identify any key words in the question and refer to them in your answer where possible.
- Keep a tight focus on the question asked, in the introduction, in the middle and at the end. Lack of focus is the main reason for low marks and grades.
- Use supporting examples and evidence to back up and develop your arguments.
- Avoid simplistic assertions, personal opinions and sweeping generalisations.
- Use political concepts, such as those identified in this guide, and political theory and vocabulary wherever possible.
- Avoid model answers based on questions set in previous papers, especially when the wording of a question has changed and a different response is required.
- Get your timing right and don't repeat points, or conclude your answer by simply repeating all you have said before. Be aware of important debates surrounding specification topics. The answer to many questions relating to American government is 'it depends', and valid arguments can be identified on both sides of the debate. Questions that ask 'how far' or 'to what extent' are alluding to those debates.
- Write with clarity and direction, with good grammar, vocabulary, spelling and legibility, to make a good overall impression on the examiner, who is going to give you a mark for your communication skills.
- GOV 4A is not a comparative paper. Marks may be gained by relevant and appropriate references to the operation of UK government to demonstrate synoptic understanding of key differences. However, high marks may be achieved without such references and they should not 'take over' the response, or be artificially introduced into each point made.

On the following pages, each question is accompanied by two exemplar answers written under timed conditions. One is of A-grade standard and the other of C-grade standard. None of the answers should be regarded as a perfect response. Each one simply represents a way of approaching the actual question set, and is followed by an indication of the grade it is likely to achieve and why.

After each of the questions, there is a section (indicated by the symbol ⓔ) identifying the focus of the question and what is expected in the answer. Each answer is followed by an examiner's comment, indicated by the symbol ⓔ: this section comments on the approach of the answer and explains some of the reasons why it has achieved the grade indicated or how a higher mark could have been gained. If you read these sections carefully, you will get an idea of how to improve your marks in the examination for both parts of the question. It will also help you become more familiar with the assessment objectives.

Question 1 The constitutional framework of US government

(a) Explain how citizens' rights are protected by the constitution in the USA.   (10 marks)

ⓔ This question calls for an explanation of the entrenched Bill of Rights, the first ten amendments to the constitution, as well as other constitutional amendments such as the 14th, guaranteeing the 'equal protection of the laws', and the protection these give to the rights of American citizens. It also expects you to show knowledge of the role of the Supreme Court in protecting citizens' rights and to include in your answer at least one or two examples of specific guaranteed constitutional rights. For the very highest marks, you could question how effective these protections actually are in modern conditions, especially since 9/11 and the war on terror.

A-grade answer

(a) In the USA, the first ten amendments to the constitution, known as the Bill of Rights, lay out the rights of the American people as citizens **a**. This is what Madison argued for when the constitution was written in 1787 **d**. The American people are very aware of their 'inalienable' rights **c**, guaranteed under the constitution, in the Bill of Rights, such as the 1st Amendment, guaranteeing personal freedoms, and later amendments which guarantee women and ethnic minorities the vote **a**.

In the USA, citizens' rights are protected in the codified constitution, which is entrenched and 'supreme law' **b**. This entrenchment ensures that the constitution is sovereign **c**, and therefore rights are guaranteed in the constitution and cannot be breached by government. Social policy from various governments has attempted to control gun crime but has faced opposition from groups such as the NRA, who refer to the 2nd Amendment, guaranteeing the right to bear arms. However, although rights are protected by the Supreme Court, it can give different interpretations over time **b**, such as saying that 'separate but equal' was constitutional in the *Plessy* case in 1896 but then reversing this ruling in the 1954 *Brown* case saying that segregation was 'inherently unequal' and therefore against the 'equal protection' clause guaranteed in the 14th Amendment. So the protection of rights can depend on the Supreme Court at the time and the cases it is willing to hear **b**.

ⓔ This student's answer **a** contains a great deal of AO1 knowledge and evidence/examples that would place it at the top of Level 4 and also **b** demonstrates excellent AO2 analysis. **c** Political vocabulary is very impressive: for example, the use of the terms 'inalienable' and 'entrenchment', which are clearly understood and used in context. **d** The reference to Madison suggests good contextual awareness. **a** There are specific references to the 1st, 2nd and 14th Amendments as evidence and **b** the role of the Supreme Court is understood vis-à-vis the protection of rights. The last sentence could have been further developed with reference to modern-day debate concerning the impact of 9/11 on rights in the USA, but the rest of the answer is of such high quality in all three assessment objectives that it would achieve a high A grade anyway.

(a) Many would argue that a codified constitution is a far better safeguard of the rights of citizens than the uncodified constitution of the UK **c**. Inspired by philosophers like John Locke, the Founding Fathers put sovereignty and liberty of the people at the very heart of the constitution **d**. In the USA the constitution and its amendments are the supreme law of the land, which no institution may ignore. The president, the Congress and the state legislatures cannot act to infringe the Bill of Rights, which contains all the rights that an individual is entitled to **a** and they are constitutionally guaranteed **c**. Though whether this is reflected in reality is open to question.

Many now argue that the US Bill of Rights has not sufficiently protected citizens from the provisions of the Patriot Act passed in 2001 and the detention without trial seen in Guantánamo Bay **b**. Also, the right to vote guaranteed to black Americans by the constitution after the Civil War was ignored by the southern states with little enforcement of those guaranteed constitutional rights by the Supreme Court **b**.

ⓔ **b** This student does challenge the effectiveness of the protections of the Bill of Rights in the last paragraph and this is worthy of AO2 credit. There is also **a** knowledge of the Bill of Rights and the 'supreme law' of the USA and **d** an impressive contextual reference to Locke. However, the first sentence is not fully explained **c** and the lack of specific examples of any of the guaranteed rights in the Bill of Rights or any other amendments is a serious omission, lowering the potential AO1 mark. Also, although it is implied, there is no explanation of the role of the Supreme Court in protecting constitutional rights. These are the reasons why this potentially very good and well-written answer would reach a very high C grade but no higher.

(b) How accurate is it to describe the US constitution as too rigid and difficult to change? (30 marks)

ⓔ This question revolves around the debate over how 'rigid' the codified US constitution actually is. It is essential that you show knowledge of the amendment procedure in your answer and perhaps the intentions of the Founding Fathers, with examples of both change and therefore 'flexibility' (with 17 amendments to choose from) but also lack of change and therefore 'rigidity' (the entrenched first ten amendments or any of the numerous failed amendments). For higher AO1 and AO2 marks you will also need to argue that change, and therefore flexibility, through 'interpretive amendments' can come through Supreme Court interpretation of the vague words of the constitution, especially from 'activist' courts such as Warren. Examples should be used of cases effectively bringing about constitutional change without any change to the document itself, showing the adaptability of the constitution to social and political developments. To gain very high marks, you should refer to the flexibility brought to the constitution by using examples of developing conventions and practices to 'fill in the gaps' where the constitution is silent.

(b) The USA has a written codified constitution and as a result it may be described as too rigid and difficult to change. The UK, by contrast, has an unwritten constitution in the sense that it is not contained in one single document so it lacks a formal constitution but is made up of a variety of different sources along with long-standing traditions **d**. This has led to some saying that it is too flexible and easy to change.

The US constitution is a written codified document, which has survived for over 200 years and is the cornerstone of American democracy and part of what it is to 'be an American'. It was intended to be a collection of fundamental principles for the new nation state. If they are such fundamental principles then it could, and possibly should, be argued that the constitution is rightfully entrenched and difficult to change **b**. When the Founding Fathers drew up the constitution they were keen to ensure that the process of amending it was relatively hard, in order to ensure political stability over the years and the longevity of the document **b**. In the USA, constitutional law is above that of ordinary statute law where there is a conflict between the two. In the UK, constitutional law does not exist, as 'constitutional changes' are implemented in exactly the same manner as statute law, by a simple majority in the sovereign Parliament, such as the devolution of power to Scotland in 1998 **d**. However, any change in power in the USA would need a constitutional amendment.

In order to amend the US constitution the Founding Fathers stated that Congress must either call a national convention at the request of two-thirds of the state legislatures or there must be a two-thirds supermajority in favour of an amendment in both houses of Congress **a**. Indeed the former has never been used. For a proposal to be ratified the Founding Fathers stipulated that there should be another supermajority in three-quarters of the state legislatures for this amendment to be added to the constitution **a**.

The relatively inflexible nature of the US constitution is revealed through the number of amendments that have been made. Since the Bill of Rights, which was the inclusion of ten inalienable rights to the constitution, there have been only 17 amendments made. Indeed two of these cancel each other out, these being the 18th and the 21st, regarding the prohibition of alcohol **a**.

While it could be argued that this is appropriate rigidity, some would argue that it prevents the USA from adapting to changes in national culture and situations. They cite the 'right to bear arms' as the principal example, highlighting the nation's failure to impose stricter gun laws **b**. However, the nature of constitutional change in the USA requires that a majority of the people put pressure on Congress to implement necessary changes. The fact that this has not happened shows that the constitution is fulfilling its role and preventing fundamental changes based on minority views, just as it was designed to do **b**.

While the limited number of amendments presents the US constitution as being highly inflexible, it has been kept up to date through judicial interpretation. The Founding Fathers granted the judiciary the power to interpret the document and this has allowed the rules of the constitution to be kept up to date **b**. It has been flexible in the sense that it can evolve along with the changes in society. In this role the judiciary has been willing to interpret the words in the light of modern conditions and ignore precedent **c**.

To conclude, while it may be argued that the US constitution is too rigid and difficult to change it must be noted that this was the desire of the Founding Fathers, as they wanted to ensure long-term political stability for America **b**. Furthermore, they set in place, using the judiciary, the ability for the constitution to be flexible in terms of its interpretation, thus allowing it to remain up to date.

(e) This very well-written response, which thus gains high AO3 marks, presents valid and convincing counter-arguments to the 'too rigid' description of the US constitution, but also defends its rigidity well, thus gaining high AO2 marks. a There is a clear understanding of the nature of constitutional rules and why they are necessary to 'ordered government'. The amendment process is competently covered and relevant examples are given, gaining high AO1 marks. c The role of the Supreme Court in interpreting the constitution, and therefore applying a new meaning to the words in it, is also highly relevant, b although examples of specific cases and different kinds of court would clarify the argument more and gain additional AO1 and AO2 marks. Nevertheless, this well-focused and structured answer has a solid conceptual understanding, never strays from the question, and d also uses some relevant synoptic comparisons with the UK constitution, so it fully deserves an A grade.

C-grade answer

(b) A constitution is a framework of rules which says how a country or governmental system should be run. It can be codified or uncodified.

The US constitution was created by the Founding Fathers in the 1700s. They created a document which would underpin America. Some argue that the constitution is out of date and should be changed for modern society c. The 'right to bear arms' is a controversial issue and is often debated after shootings such as those at Virginia Tech. So far this has not been changed as many citizens see this as their constitutional right a c.

To make an amendment to the constitution, three-quarters of states need to agree a. This process is lengthy and often unsuccessful. This is how the Founding Fathers wanted it to be c.

However, it is also argued that the US constitution is vague and therefore open to interpretation, as the Supreme Court does regularly a. Depending on the nature of the court, the constitution is interpreted in different ways. The 1953–69 Warren Court was loose constructionist and many controversial rulings were made, such as *Brown* v *Topeka Board of Education* a c. This key ruling stopped segregation in schools.

Amendments have been made to the constitution. The Bill of Rights is fundamental to US government and lays down the rights of citizens. The US constitution has evolved over time c.

In the UK there is no formal document and Parliament is sovereign, laying down rules and practices. Any Acts passed by Parliament are to be followed. This shows it is easy to change the uncodified constitution by passing a law. Unlike the US constitution, there is no room for interpretation or vagueness. The UK constitution does evolve, however, which means it is not outdated to the extent of the US constitution d.

It is clear that on the surface the US constitution may appear unchangeable but this is not the case. It is vague enough to allow interpretation by the courts. This in turn allows it to evolve and be applied to modern society b. Although the amendment process is rigid, it prevents maverick laws being passed c and the constitution being overrun with amendments. It is, however, harder to change than the UK constitution due to its codified form.

ⓔ Although this answer is basically sound in some of its knowledge and analysis, therefore gaining some **a** AO1 and **b** AO2 marks, **c** there is far too much vagueness around many of the arguments and statements, such as 'The US constitution has evolved over time' or 'this process is lengthy and not always successful', and they are not developed or backed up with supporting evidence. In addition, the amendment process is not fully understood or explained and there are no examples of the passage of, or failure to pass, amendments to demonstrate either flexibility or the lack of it. The argument relating to the 2nd Amendment is not well expressed. Similarly, the role of the Supreme Court in constitutional interpretation is understood but undeveloped. There is much assertion in the response but the student does not back it up with clear evidence. What is meant by 'codified'? What is a 'loose constructionist' court? What does the student mean by 'maverick laws'? However, the answer does have some focus and **d** introduces relevant comparisons with the UK which are more convincing than the arguments relating to the USA. As a result, it would achieve a C grade but could have been much higher with better-developed explanations and supporting evidence and examples.

Question 2 The legislative branch of government: US Congress

> **(a) How important is party as an influence over congressional voting behaviour?**   (10 marks)

ⓔ To answer this question you need to evaluate the varying influences that affect congressional voting while focusing on party as just one of these influences. You should explain why party is a relatively weak influence on members of Congress (when compared to MPs in the UK Parliament) but also for marks at the higher level demonstrate knowledge that recent changes in Congress may have led to the greater significance of party voting than in the past, giving some explanation of this too. For higher marks, and to address the 'how important' part of the question, you will also need to identify other factors influencing congressional voting, such as constituents or pressure groups.

> **A-grade answer**

(a) It is a generally held view that parties are much looser and thus hold less influence in the American Congress than they do in the UK Parliament and this does seem to be the case.

In the USA, parties are not as clear-cut as in the UK and there are many reasons for this **b**. One in particular is the fact that the USA is a huge and very diverse country. Thus it would be difficult for a party with a rigid ideology to claim support from all areas of the country. A classic example of this would be the southern democrats. During the 1950s and 60s, the southern democrats were at their most prominent, and although they were members of the Democratic Party they were very right wing, e.g. anti civil rights, yet the Democratic Party is more liberal and to the left of the Republican Party. This lack of cohesion shows parties have little influence on congressmen **a b**. Voting in Congress is more influenced by regional issues and the needs of members' particular states and districts. Congressmen 'pork-barrel' to 'bring home the bacon' to the 'folks back home' to help them gain re-election **a b**. Voting is also influenced by pressure groups, which may help to finance re-election campaigns, which the party does not do **a b**.

The lack of a promotion structure (as in the UK from back bench to front bench), because of the separation of powers, means that there is little that a party can offer its members **a b c**. Also, congressmen can't rely on their party to get them re-elected as elections occur through primaries in which individual personality and personal views are by far the most important factors in electoral success **b**.

That said, the speaker of the House of Representatives and the majority party leaders have influence over committee membership, which holds a higher status in Congress **a**. Also, perhaps the USA is set to change. In 1994 it saw the first Republican victory in the House and Senate for 40 years. To consolidate this, the speaker of the House, Newt Gingrich, used the 'Contract with America' to galvanise the Republicans and make them a more cohesive conservative party under his leadership. This led to higher levels of party voting than had been the case previously **a b**. The Democratic Party in Congress has also lost its deeply conservative southern wing, who were rare party voters, and as a result the Democratic Party also has more cohesion when voting on issues **a b**.

However, the parties in Congress lack the party cohesion and loyalty of the UK parliamentary parties, with their vigorous whipping system, party discipline and the 'carrots of ministerial office', which cannot be used in the Congress to keep party voting in line **b c**. In the UK, most voters vote for the party and its manifesto, not for the individual as in most US elections **c**.

So, in conclusion, the party is simply one factor in influencing votes in Congress and is not necessarily the most important one **d**.

🅔 This answer is fully focused on the question throughout, **a** showing excellent AO1 knowledge and contextual understanding of the influences on congressional voting, and **b** it develops several lines of analysis for high AO2 marks, showing why party may not be a strong factor affecting voting. **c** The comparison with the UK shows synoptic understanding. There is excellent evidence relating to recent changes in party cohesion, such as the impact of the 1994 Contract with America and the loss of the Democratic Party's southern wing, showing increasing partisanship. Other influences on voting are included and assessed, and **d** a short but necessary conclusion is given, leading to a high A grade for this comprehensive answer.

C-grade answer

(a) Party can play an important role in influencing the actions of members of Congress, providing a loyalty which often affects the way they vote **a**.

However, the primary influence on the way congressmen vote is loyalty to their constituents and they vote in Congress to gain concessions for their constituency with the aim of 'bringing home the pork' via cross-party voting **a**.

In the UK Parliament, MPs are primarily concerned with party loyalty and backbench rebellions are rare, with MPs often described as 'lobby fodder' for their parties because of the strong whip system and party discipline. At the extreme, de-selection can be threatened and career prospects damaged **c**. By contrast, the 'bargaining process' that takes place in Congress on votes creates a far less adversarial system than in the UK, and members of Congress from different parties often vote together on issues **a b**. In the USA, the separation of powers reduces the sense of party reliance and loyalty, as the president cannot offer jobs to members of Congress in return for their loyalty and support **a**. The weak party system in Congress also means that there are no sanctions that can be used to persuade members of Congress to vote with their parties **a b**. As a result they are not 'loyal' to their party in Congress and are not 'lobby fodder' for their parties.

ⓔ a This answer addresses the specific question, and makes some attempt to explain congressional voting, but **b** it lacks specific AO1 evidence and examples of any of the other factors that affect the way a member of Congress votes, being far too vague and undeveloped throughout. **c** Although synoptic references to the UK would be rewarded, the answer does stray a little too far towards explaining the UK system, thereby failing to use the available time to focus attention on congressional voting, with party as just one variable affecting this. More explanation as to why members of Congress have weak party ties, plus why they may have closer ties to the 'folks back home' and to interest groups, would lift this answer from a C grade into a low B.

(b) Critically evaluate the role and activities of congressional committees.   (30 marks)

ⓔ This question demands a critical evaluation for high AO2 marks, not simply a description of what the powerful congressional committees do. You will need to cover their role within Congress vis-à-vis the executive branch of government and show knowledge and understanding of how committees actually operate in Congress within the legislative and oversight processes. You will be expected to include examples of these roles and processes, in both the House and Senate. Knowledge of why the congressional committees are so powerful is essential to your response, but you should keep a clear focus on the criticisms made of their role and power within the separation of powers system and the resulting checks and balances. These could be the gridlock of the legislative process, or the failure of oversight due to iron triangles. You could legitimately refer to the much weaker UK parliamentary select committees to demonstrate understanding gained from your AS studies.

A-grade answer

(b) Woodrow Wilson once said that the USA had 'government by the chairmen of the standing committees'. He was frustrated by the power of these committees and is one of a long line of people to criticise the influence they are able to exert over both legislation and the actions of the executive branch of government. All senators and congressmen sit on at least one committee and they are seen as a very important part of a politician's legislative and oversight duty **a**. The standing committees are responsible for overseeing a particular area of government (such as agriculture or veterans' affairs) and the members of the committee are permanent (due to the incumbency effect in US politics, they often sit on that committee for a number of years), which means that they gain expert knowledge in the field that they operate in and are well placed to tackle the executive and to check and balance its power **a b**.

The president is detached from both the legislature and the law-making process, so he relies on his allies in Congress to push legislation through for him. However, it is the chairmen of the standing committees who have the final say over whether a piece of legislation is adopted by the committee for discussion. Only if it is adopted can it pass through the relevant legislative process in order to be made a law **a**. The committee has the power to summon anyone to come and give evidence to it, and as its debates and activities are often televised it can gain a huge amount of media attention and, therefore, power **b**. It is in these committees that politicians are said to forge their reputation and they pork-barrel here to gain amendments to legislation that will please their constituents (but not the president) and help their re-election. This is a criticised part of the committees' activities as it leads to very high spending **b**.

US committees can also form strong bonds with pressure groups that reflect their area of interest and also the federal departments that they monitor. This three-way symbiotic relationship is known as an 'iron triangle' **e**. President Nixon is said to have felt the power of these ties when he attempted to move the education of veterans from the control of the Veterans' Agency to the Department of Education. The agency resisted the move, the American Legion and other veterans' interest groups opposed the move, and the standing congressional Veterans' Affairs Committee condemned the decision and would not support it. President Nixon backed down **b**.

US congressional committees also have a lot of investigative powers, such as over the Iran–Contra affair and the Watergate scandal in the past and the recent committees investigating 9/11 and the 2008 banking crisis. It was probably the investigative role of congressional committees that brought down President Nixon for his role in the Watergate affair **a b f**.

However, the power of these organisations can be defended. Surely it is only right that members of Congress possess an expertise over certain areas of policy (indeed organisations such as the CBO, the Congressional Budget Office, have been set up to encourage this expertise within the legislature) so that Congress can more effectively check and balance the power of the executive branch. It is better that congressmen and senators who have a broad knowledge of all areas of policy, but are specialists in none, develop this expertise during their time in Congress **c**.

Also, with the weak party system in Congress, it may be argued that it is necessary that congressmen and senators use their legislative and oversight power on committees and form 'voting blocks' by which they can most effectively exercise their own power and democratic mandate from the people who elected them **c**. Furthermore, a symbiotic working relationship between a federal department, congressional committee and relevant interest groups can be seen as a way to take all views into account and create acceptable, well-thought-out policy **c**. With the federal government extending into people's lives as never before, it may be seen as desirable to have powerful organisations keeping a check on its every move **c**.

In the UK, standing and select committees are relatively weak, and the reputation of politicians is made on the floor of the House of Commons not in committees, unlike in the USA. Parliamentary committees are dominated to some degree by the executive, as their membership is chosen by the executive and the majority party has a major influence on how they work **d**. The difference between the two countries can be seen in the reaction to intelligence failures, which were implicated in the decision to go to war in Iraq. The Foreign Relations standing committee in the US Congress used its full power and publicity to condemn major figures in the administration (which, in part, led to Karl Rove's resignation). The Foreign Affairs select committee in the UK had very little impact or media coverage **d**. This means that in the USA the executive branch operates in conditions where it knows that its moves will be checked and its legislation will not pass unless thoroughly scrutinised by committees of Congress. Although much of the president's agenda may be blocked here, at least there is no 'executive dominance' as found in the Westminster Parliament **d**.

ⓔ **a** This answer demonstrates many of the workings of congressional committees in both legislative activity and oversight, thus raising the AO1 mark, and is a comprehensive and focused response to the question. **b** It demonstrates excellent AO2 analytical skills and depth of understanding of congressional committees, and strong contextual awareness of their role and activities. **c** Counter-views are also very effectively covered as the student defends the power of the congressional committees in a highly evaluative way. **f** Impressive examples are deployed and **d** synoptic comparisons are effectively made with some of the weaknesses of UK committees. **e** In addition, the use of impressive political vocabulary, such as the coverage of iron triangles, and the overall coherence of the response make this answer worthy of a high A grade.

C-grade answer

(b) Standing committees in the Congress are more powerful and perform much more important roles than their UK counterparts. In the USA, standing committee stage comes after the first reading of the bill and before the second reading. In that stage, the standing committee has the power to decide whether or not the bill goes on to the second reading. Due to the large amount of bills coming before Congress, that is a very important function. (In the UK, standing committee would come after the second reading, where the main principles of the bill would have already been discussed. So committees don't have much power to influence the construction of a bill like in the USA **d**.)

In the US system the committee stage of the bill is the most important part, as it consists of the policy specialists who consider the bill first and make all necessary amendments to it. They have the power to influence the substance of the bill by going through each point. Both UK and US standing committees would involve interest groups in the discussions on the bill **a**.

US committees, as Bennett would argue, are more high-profile bodies, and are independent from the executive. This means that a president wouldn't be able to directly influence the outcome of the committee, unlike in the UK where committee members are influenced by the executive **c**.

The US standing committees are said to be the main bodies inside Congress which actually legislate. Their power is enormous. They are the bodies which have close links with pressure groups and, therefore, this gives them extra power and prestige **c**. Also, US standing committees have the very important role of scrutinising the executive, in addition to their legislative power. They can summon any executive member and have investigations into the executive's actions **a**. As members of US committees are independent from the executive, it creates the environment for objective accountability **b**. US committees are also highly financed. This is explained by the importance of their work and the scale of it, as most of the work is done there **c**.

However, US committees are not totally powerful. Whatever they come up with in a bill has to be discussed by Congress. Even if it is approved it still has to go through final stages where two versions of the bill are compared by both chambers. The president would ultimately have the power to decide whether this bill becomes law or not (even though he can be overridden).

Standing committees in the Senate also have the power to approve the appointments made by the president **a**, which further shows their power and influence in the US system.

🅔 The first paragraph does not start this essay well. Confusion over 'standing committee stages' inhibits the development of a coherent response to the question. An introductory paragraph discussing why the congressional committees are so powerful in the USA (perhaps compared to their UK counterparts) would provide more focus and would serve as the starting point of an answer containing critical evaluation. This is introduced later into the answer, but it is done almost as an afterthought. However, **a** the student does demonstrate some AO1 knowledge and understanding of congressional committees and their role in legislation and oversight, although **c** a lot of the answer is rather vague and lacking supporting evidence or detail: for example, knowledge of the Conference Committee is only implied and there is no explanation of why links with pressure groups 'give them extra power'. **d** There is a brief synoptic reference to the parliamentary committees in the UK, which is creditable but not especially informative. **b** Other references to congressional committees, their resources and the Senate committees with confirmation power over presidential appointments are implied and gain some credit, but they are never developed enough to gain higher AO1 or AO2 marks. The answer is therefore worth a C grade, but with further developed explanations of the role and power of congressional committees, and examples of specific committees and their legislative or oversight activities, it could have achieved a solid B.

Question 3 The executive branch of government

(a) What factors does a president consider when choosing his cabinet? (10 marks)

ⓔ Cabinet construction is one of the first and most important tasks of an incoming president distributing the 'spoils of office'. Without a shadow cabinet to draw upon, the president has many personal and political factors to take into account when constructing a cabinet that will be acceptable to Congress, especially the Senate, his party and the country. The more factors you can discuss in the time available to demonstrate your knowledge of this process, along with supporting evidence from recent presidential selections, the higher your likely AO1 and AO2 mark.

A-grade answer

(a) The cabinet in the USA is by no means as important or powerful as its UK equivalent. The cabinet in the USA is an advisory body, not a decision-taking one, and this will certainly affect the president's choices **a**. The president must bear in mind the need for Senate confirmation of his nominees so he cannot make too controversial a choice as they may be rejected, as George Bush's choice for defense secretary, John Tower, was in 1989 **b**.

When creating the cabinet, a US president looks for specialist knowledge and competence in the field of the federal department each person will represent **a**. For example, Tom Vilsack, the current agriculture secretary, was governor of Iowa a key agricultural state. As a result he is only in the cabinet for agriculture holding no other post and not moving positions. In the UK, cabinet ministers are selected for their political capabilities rather than expertise, as they are frequently reshuffled. Presidents must concentrate on how they will get good policy advice, while prime ministers are more concerned with political characteristics and party support **c**. In the USA, cabinet members are not rivals to the president and have no power base of their own.

Another factor taken into account by the president is the demographic make-up of the country and he may want to give broader appeal to his administration by making it more diverse and representative **a**. This is not always the case, however, as Nixon's cabinet was said to be 'a dozen grey-haired men called George' **b**. Clinton, on the other hand, wanted the cabinet to 'look like America' in terms of racial and gender factors **a b**. This can, however, be difficult due to the limited sources of cabinet members, who are often outgoing congressmen or previous holders of influential positions. As a result of the fact that they must be experts in their field, it is difficult for presidents to create a culturally diverse cabinet, even if they want to **b**.

As the US cabinet is only advisory to the president, it is less important for the president to fill it with political allies **a**. It is usually said that presidents have a free hand when choosing, but often they have political considerations to take into account too. Obama had to offer his main rival in the primaries, Hillary Clinton, an important job (secretary of state) in his first administration. **b**. However, all cabinet members must share the president's political objectives. Almost all cabinet members leave their posts when the president leaves office.

ⓔ **a** This is a fully focused answer, covering at least four factors influencing presidential choice, with examples and evidence given. **b** Four different presidents are referred to, together with the reasons for their cabinet choices, thus scoring very high AO1 and AO2 marks. There is a strong understanding of the operation of the US cabinet itself (for example, that it is simply an advisory body) that comes through clearly in the answer, which is very well constructed. **c** There are also appropriate synoptic references to the UK cabinet. This answer reaches the top of Level 4 for both AO1 and AO2 marks as it is 'excellent' and 'comprehensive', and would achieve a high A grade.

C-grade answer

(a) There are several factors that must be taken into account by the president, as head of government, when he is creating his cabinet. The most prominent is the specific balance achieved within the cabinet. For example, the regional and political balance **a** must be levelled to a degree that would satisfy both parties **b**, due to the need for support from both parties to push through legislation and to confirm the appointments made **b**. For example, Bill Clinton, a moderate Democrat, chose to sustain this balance by appointing Al Gore as his vice-president, another moderate.

Other factors taken into consideration include appointing a figure as a reward for support given in the past, for example in the election campaign **a**, and, due to the vast recruitment pool available in the US, the president looks for specialist status and some kind of expertise in a certain policy field connected to the cabinet post itself **a**.

ⓔ **a** The inclusion of two or three relevant points, covering cabinet 'balance' and policy expertise, gains some AO1 marks but **b** most analysis is simply implied, therefore failing to gain potential AO2 marks. This answer just manages to scrape into the bottom of a C grade but it is a very limited response to the question. **a** No argument is fully developed, such as what is meant by 'regional' or 'political' balance. The only example given is incorrect, that of Al Gore being selected as vice-president. The selection of a vice-president is done before the election, not as a cabinet post.

(b) Discuss the view that the president is at his most powerful in his first 2 years of office. (30 marks)

ⓔ This question is focused on the importance of the so-called 'honeymoon period' of a presidency. A good answer would not only contain a wide range of examples to support the view, but also consider alternative views and interpretations. The role of unexpected events, whether Congress is controlled by his party and the ever-present powers of the veto and signing statements, could also be included to produce a balanced answer. In essence, candidates would be expected to largely agree with the view put forward, but to explain their case convincingly with accurate supporting evidence and also to take into account other lines of analysis.

(b) The US president has a wide range of powers both formal (laid down in the constitution) and informal (e.g. Neudstat's power to persuade) **a**, but arguably all of these powers are most effective during the first 2 years before the mid-term elections when presidents often suffer losses as Obama did in 2010. There are, however, some qualifications to this analysis as will be discussed later.

The main reason why the first 2 years, especially the first 100 days or 'honeymoon period', is when a president is at his most powerful is due to the momentum from his election victory and the mandate that gives him. Therefore presidents try to pass the most important parts of their legislative program as soon as possible. George W. Bush did this with education (NCLB) in 2000, and Obama with his healthcare reforms in 2010 **b**. They are more likely to have a 'friendly' Congress at the start of their presidency as there is often a knock-on effect on congressional elections (tailcoat effect) **c** at the time of the national presidential election. By contrast, many presidents, such as Bush in 2006 and Obama in 2010, see their party lose ground in mid-term elections **c** which often leads to divided government, which in turn makes legislation harder to pass. Members of his own party in Congress are also more willing to cooperate with a president in his first 2 years as they may want his help and support in their own re-election bids. By contrast, during the 'lame duck' period, even members of his own party may refuse to back the president on policy initiatives as there is little he can do to help them in return. It is worth noting though, that it does depend on the size of the president's election victory — Bush was in a relatively weak position following the very close and controversial election of 2000. Obama's relatively weak re-election margin in 2012 also reduced his standing with some of Congress, perhaps explaining why some Democrats felt able to oppose publicly airstrikes on Syria in 2013 **d**.

Presidents also appear stronger in their first couple of years because that is when they need to get their cabinet (and some other executive positions) confirmed by Congress. Although there is often some lively debate, most presidents get their nominations through without a major problem or defeat. The last veto of a president's nominee to the cabinet was that of John Tower back in 1989. The first 2 years are when a president dispenses most of his powers of patronage and appointment. However, arguably the most important power a president can wield long term is that of appointing to the Supreme Court. These vacancies can occur at any stage (or indeed never, as was the case with Carter) of a president's term of office, and can have a lasting impact for years to come, the so-called 'echo chamber' effect. Some have said that Bush's most powerful legacy and power was his ability to tilt the court in a more conservative direction by replacing a moderate 'swing' justice Sandra Day O'Connor with a more conservative one, Alito.

There are, however, some other qualifications **e** to be made to the general rule that a president is at his most powerful in the first 2 years in office. Events such as 9/11 or the assassination of Osama bin Laden if handled well can boost presidents' poll ratings and make them more powerful. In the area of foreign policy especially, it could be argued that as commander in chief, a president's power is fairly consistent throughout his term in office even if a popular president is likely to have a more compliant Congress. Obama's handling of Hurricane Sandy, which was right at the end of his first term, was generally widely praised and helped boost his re-election chances. By contrast, Bush's perceived poor handling of Hurricane Katrina made him look weak and inept. Events can occur at any stage in a president's term of office and how a president handles them can be crucial to his power, or at least to the perception of that power.

The powers of veto and signing statements **f** are also important weapons in a president's armoury, and again can (and are) equally powerful at any stage during his term in office. Interestingly though, as Bush junior encountered, vetoes are more likely to be overturned towards the end of a president's term in office.

Overall therefore, while it is largely true that a president is most powerful in the period between inauguration and the mid-terms, especially when it comes to passing the legislative program, there are some powers that remain constant such as the veto and executive orders. Circumstances and the handling of crises also impact on their powers.

🅔 **a** This answer is well focused from the start, and although an introduction is not crucial to the top grade, here it works well by providing relevant context and some effective understanding of both the formal and informal nature of presidential powers. The introduction also shows a clear analytical understanding of the main thrust of the question and suggests the general line of approach, namely agreeing with the statement while seeing the limits to it as well.

In the second paragraph, the most important point is clearly identified and is then supported by key examples **b** from recent presidencies, which would gain marks for AO2. There is good evidence of synopticity as well when the answer shows an awareness of the power of Congress over legislation and the importance of united government in helping a president, as well as brief but relevant reference to voting behaviour **c** — a GOVP3 topic but one that would still be credited. This would gain marks for AO1 and AO3. The paragraph also includes an intelligent counter-example **d** at the end, again drawing on recent events to make a convincing approach. There is also very good analysis of patronage powers, again supported by effective examples in the next paragraph, and an intelligent analysis of the other side of the argument **e**. All this would gain marks for AO2. Although the powers of executive orders and signing statements are not really developed in any great length **f**, the quality of the powers that are fully analysed and the balanced response provided, would make this a secure A-grade answer.

C-grade answer

(b) The president of the USA has numerous powers. Some of these are: the powers of appointment, the veto and signing statements, the 'bully pulpit' and the power to persuade. Their powers often depend, however, on time and circumstance as well what is formally in the constitution. Presidential power is rather like the tide in that it ebbs and flows **e**. Bush was very unpopular and thus quite weak immediately after his narrow and disputed win in 2000, but his handling of 9/11 made him very popular and increased his power considerably. Presidents often seek to get their manifesto promises **d** passed in the first 2 years before they do badly in the mid-terms, e.g. 2012, which leads often to divided government and makes laws hard to pass. Obama got Obamacare through before 2012 therefore, and Bush did the same with education soon after 2000 **a**.

Presidents also have the power of patronage and normally wield this at the start when they appoint their cabinet, but can if they are lucky, appoint Supreme Court judges at any time if one dies or retires, e.g. John Paul Stevens in 2010. They also have the power of veto and issuing executive orders, which they can do at any time, although Obama has issued the lowest number of vetoes of any president to date. These powers are there throughout their term in office and are not really most powerful in the first 2 years **b**.

Presidential power is also about handling crises and events — the better a president handles a problem, the more his power and prestige increases. While Obama got credit for handling Hurricane Sandy well, Bush by contrast was widely attacked for how badly he mishandled Hurricane Katrina **a**. Where a president is in his term of office thus has little impact on how he manages problems **b**.

The first 100 days is also known as the 'honeymoon period' when presidents normally have a lot of goodwill and support especially from Congress **c**. Members of their party are much less likely to oppose presidents then, and tend to support their policies and bills, though the Democrat-controlled Senate did reject Obama's attempts to curb gun sales after the recent school shootings **a**. So presidents do not always get their own way with Congress. This may also be because they are not good at what is known as the 'power to persuade', which is about their personal skills and character rather than where they are in terms of their presidency. Good presidents will use their charm and offers of hospitality (White House BBQs etc.) to try to win over members of the Senate or House to support their bills or point of view. They also use the media and State of the Union address to put forward their views, sometimes known as the 'bully pulpit'. A president who is an effective communicator, e.g. Reagan, will often be more effective than a poor media performer.

Overall, the statement is largely true; a president is much more powerful at the start than at the end of his term in office. However, some of his powers, e.g. veto and persuasion are there throughout his presidency.

🄴 This answer, although quite knowledgeable in parts and including several references to recent events **a**, is not completely focused on the actual question. It is a rather general survey of presidential powers with some attempt at direct linkage **b** often at the end of a paragraph. This will gain some credit for AO2 but it would have been better to be focused much more consistently on the question. The answer also suffers from a rather weak structure with much of the material in the penultimate paragraph **c** being better suited to the earlier sections of the answer. This would make it hard to justify a high mark for AO3. Also note the inaccurate use of political vocabulary when mention is made of a manifesto **d**, which is a term more reserved for UK politics. There is also some vagueness of understanding **e** when describing the fluctuating nature of presidential power, which would need proper explanation and development to gain high marks for AO1. Overall, the answer is knowledgeable and relevant enough to merit a C grade, but could easily be improved by a better structure, and more development of some of the points that it makes. It would also have helped if the candidate addressed the notion of the first 2 years much sooner in the answer.

Question 4 The judicial branch of government: the Supreme Court

(a) Explain the criteria by which a president selects candidates for the Supreme Court. (10 marks)

Ⓔ This question requires knowledge of the main requirements for Supreme Court nominations. A good answer should focus on the range of factors that will be present, including not only the judicial philosophy of prospective nominees but also the more practical factors, such as getting a nomination through the Senate and evidence of legal expertise at a high level. For high marks it is essential to quote several examples, including perhaps cases of failed nominations, to support the overall case being made. Note that the question is not specifically about the process by which candidates for the Supreme Court are appointed, which is a slightly different question.

A-grade answer

(a) **a** The appointment of Supreme Court justices is one of the most important powers a US president can have since their tenure for life makes them something of an 'echo chamber'. It is therefore vital that the president makes the 'right' choice, and so to enable this, he will be looking for a number of key criteria **d**. Perhaps the most important factor **e** will be the judicial philosophy or outlook of a nominee. Democrat presidents since the war have generally favoured more activist or loose constructionist **c** justices who will be more favourable to establishing new rights in areas such as abortion or civil rights. Obama's two nominees so far, Kagan and Sotomayor **b**, are both regarded as being on the liberal wing of the court. By contrast, Republicans tend to prefer strict constructionists who favour judicial restraint. Bush Junior therefore appointed Alito and Roberts, who are generally regarded as conservatives **b**. However, another key criteria is that the nominee must be capable of getting confirmed by the Senate on a simple majority vote. Reagan, for example, saw his favoured nominee, Robert Bork, rejected because he was seen as being too conservative. Bush had to withdraw the nomination of Miers as she was seen as being too inexperienced **b**. This factor has become increasingly important as confirmation hearings have become more politicised over recent years. Finally, it is vital that the nominee is deemed 'legally qualified' and to possess the necessary legal qualifications — the most recent nomination, Elena Kagan, had been a law professor at Harvard and also served as solicitor general, while Chief Justice Roberts had previously served as an appeal court judge **c**. In summary, a nominee must reflect the president's own judicial preference and outlook (some have 'disappointed', e.g. Earl Warren) but also be suitably experienced and capable of getting through the Senate confirmation process.

Ⓔ **a** Although the answer starts off slightly generally, in fact this mini introduction sets up the answer well. It is not vital to a high grade answer but in this case works by briefly placing the answer in context. It is perhaps obvious, but nonetheless sensible, to mention the existence of several factors **d**, but what is especially effective is to introduce a degree of prioritisation of factors

e, which would gain AO2 marks. The answer makes use of several recent examples **b** when discussing the three main factors, which would gain high marks for AO1 — mention of Kagan and Robert's previous posts shows impressively detailed knowledge. There is also use of political vocabulary **c**. Overall, the answer is well structured and consistently focused on the question making it worthy of a high A grade.

C-grade answer

(a) Not all presidents have the opportunity to appoint Supreme Court judges, e.g. Carter, while some such as Bush and Obama have appointed two **a**. They have to get their appointments through the Senate Judiciary Committee **d**, which can be tricky as Reagan found with Bork. However, Obama got his two choices through — Kagan and Sotomayor **b**. They also want to pick a candidate who is of their political persuasion, so Democrats pick liberals **d** while Republicans pick conservatives/judicial restraint.

They also need to choose someone who is 'up to the job' **c** and is deemed 'legally well qualified'; this is not always the case, e.g. Bush and Miers. So overall a president has to pick his candidates carefully and bear in mind a number of factors.

🄴 **a** The first paragraph begins in a rather unfocused way, with a statement which while true does not lead on to set up the answer to the question. There is some accurate knowledge here of recent nominations **b**, which would gain credit for AO2, but elsewhere **d** knowledge is rather vague and/ or inaccurate. While it is true that the Senate Judiciary Committee is important in the confirmation process, the answer would be enhanced if mention had also made of the need to get through the whole Senate as well. It is a pity that the valid point about legal qualifications is not backed up by an example or two, and no direct reference is made of the ABA rating to which the term 'well qualified' refers. It is also wise to avoid colloquialisms **c**, which does not really enhance the answer. Overall, the answer has enough knowledge and range of factors to make it mid-range, but would benefit from a greater development of the points raised, and from a tighter, more fluent structure.

(b) 'Politicians sitting on a bench'. How accurate is this description of the US Supreme Court?   (30 marks)

🄴 The question is referring to the debate surrounding the politicisation of the judicial branch of government and the extent of its 'political' as opposed to its 'judicial' role. Your answer will need to include analysis relating to the appointment process of justices, with examples of controversial political appointments, the political importance of the court's power of judicial review and the judicial philosophies of activism and restraint and the 'loose' and 'strict' constructionism of constitutional interpretation, with examples from landmark cases, or different courts, to show evidence (or not) of any politicisation of the Supreme Court.

A-grade answer

(b) The description is suggesting that members of the Supreme Court are 'politicians' rather than justices and this is open to debate.

In the USA, the Supreme Court was set up by the constitution and the justices are senior members of the judiciary, usually with vast legal experience. It is the appointment process of these justices, and the role that they play, which may lead to them being described as 'politicians'. In the USA the process has been described as highly politicised, with the president nominating a nominee and the Senate confirming the nomination **a b**. One nominee, Samuel Alito, had a difficult nomination and his experience tested by the Judiciary Committee in the Senate with lots of media attention given to it, demonstrating the importance of the Supreme Court and the belief that Bush nominated Alito to please the conservative right of his supporters **b**.

Presidents generally nominate people who are likely to reflect their ideological views on the court. However, Eisenhower nominated Chief Justice Earl Warren as a conservative but the Warren Court's decisions turned out to be the most liberal in the court's history **a**.

Apart from looking at the appointment process, which seems to be more overtly political in the USA than in the UK, although that could be due to the physical separation of the Supreme Court from the other branches, one can also look at the roles, functions and powers of the judiciary to see whether their actions suggest that they are really 'politicians' and not judges.

The Supreme Court's jurisdiction is laid out in Article 3 of the constitution. However, after the 1803 *Marbury* v *Madison* and 1819 *McCulloch* v *Maryland* cases, precedents were set concerning judicial review. In accordance with these two cases the Supreme Court could rule as to whether state legislatures or the federal government were acting unconstitutionally **b**. This precedent has remained out of respect for the sovereignty of the constitution and places the Supreme Court at the heart of decision making, and the court has struck down over 700 state laws and 80 federal laws as unconstitutional, thus overruling the elected bodies **a b**. Other rulings show that the Supreme Court is a body which can have much 'political' influence. The case of *Roe* v *Wade* in 1973 and subsequent cases concerned abortion and the *Brown* v *Board of Education of Topeka* case led to the end of segregation — decisions that could be deemed to be 'political'. The recent verdict on gay rights (*Perry* v *Hollingsworth*) also supports this view. On the other hand, it could be argued that these decisions were based on the interpretation of the words of the constitution. However, the tendency for most justices to rule according to the ideology they believe in, and the change that comes about from the court reinterpreting decisions, suggest these rulings are indeed political, and they certainly have political consequences **b**.

Similarly, the Supreme Court ensures that civil rights and liberties are fully protected with a contextual interpretation of the constitution, known as loose construction, of the words of the constitution in the modern context **d**, such as the cases seen above. The court even decided the outcome of the 2000 election in the *Bush* v *Gore* case when it ruled that the recount of ballots in Florida was unconstitutional, which many saw as a 'political' decision by justices appointed by past Republican presidents. However, the court has to wait for cases to come before it and not all cases will be heard **a**.

The Supreme Court has gone through periods of both judicial activism **c**, such as the Warren Court where it made more 'liberal' rulings, but also periods of judicial restraint **c** when it refused to hear cases and was regarded as a more conservative court. It is regarded as being more 'political' with the former rather than the latter.

American people see the justices on the court as their judicial and constitutional representatives acting as a check on the other branches of government and protecting their rights and liberties. In the UK, the Law Lords' verdicts using judicial review also have political consequences, such as the recent ban on evidence obtained from torture, but this was not perceived as being anti-Labour **d**. In contrast, the decisions the Supreme Court reaches on politically controversial issues like abortion seem to arise more from the justices' political views rather than their reading of the constitution itself, hence 'politicians sitting on a bench'.

(e) This answer is very focused on the question and keeps the focus throughout the essay. It is a comprehensive response in both **a** AO1 and **b** AO2 assessment objectives, covering a lot of ground in relation to the appointment process and the importance of judicial review, through to discussion of judicial philosophy and different kinds of court, such as liberal or conservative, activist or restrained. **c** The political language and vocabulary used is impressive and the essay shows clear understanding not only of the judicial role of the Supreme Court but also of the reasons why it is often accused of having a more political role. This means high marks for all three assessment objectives. **d** Excellent evidence and examples are also given from cases decided by the court, such as *Brown*, *Roe* and *Bush* v *Gore* as well as more recent cases. Some reference is made to the UK Law Lords, demonstrating progression from AS. This is a well-argued A-grade response, although a more convincing conclusion could have been drawn.

C-grade answer

(b) In the USA it is generally accepted that Supreme Court justices are somewhat political especially when compared to the Law Lords in the UK. Supreme Court justices are appointed by the president but only if the Senate approves their appointment **a**. The Senate approval of the judges is a way of making sure that the Supreme Court does not become too biased towards one political viewpoint. There was a controversial debate in the USA as to who would replace Sandra Day O'Connor. The president (G. W. Bush) hoped that his choice, Sam Alito, would be approved. However, this would mean the Supreme Court would be biased towards the conservatives. Alito is considered a hard-line conservative but Sandra Day O'Connor was considered a 'swing vote'. This is an example of the legislative wing acting as a barrier to the Supreme Court becoming too politically biased. In the UK, Law Lords used to be appointed by the prime minister, but appointments were not made because of their political views but because of their experience and reputation.

US Supreme Court justices are appointed for life. This means that a president rarely gets to choose more than one justice, if any at all **a**. This is another way in which the court is stopped from becoming politically biased; because the justices remain the same from government to government it generally means that when the time comes to appoint a new judge the same president isn't in power and often it is a different party to the last time, meaning opinions in the executive and legislative wings will have changed and the Supreme Court will not be manipulated towards either a strong conservative or liberal majority.

There are examples of judges in the USA effectively making law and in some cases changing the constitution. In these cases, for example *Roe* v *Wade*, the political bias of the court is extremely important. In *Roe* v *Wade* the right to abortion was challenged: Mrs Roe, who resided in Texas, wanted the right to have an abortion, which was illegal at that time. The case went to the Supreme Court and it was up to the court to decide whether or not to change the law on abortion. The outcome was that the liberal judges won and the law was changed to allow abortion in all the states; however, the states did not have to, and still do not have to, fund abortion clinics. This is a clear example of political bias in the Supreme Court having an impact on citizens and does somewhat support the claim that the Supreme Court justices are 'politicians sitting on a bench'.

The United States judiciary are more politicised than the Law Lords in the UK. When a president has to appoint a justice he will try as hard as possible to get a judge in who will tip the balance of the Supreme Court towards their own and their party's views **b**. In the UK judges are appointed for different reasons and political opinion rarely comes into it. The Supreme Court judges are 'politicians sitting on a bench' to a substantial degree.

(e) This essay, although at times **a** quite knowledgeable and focused, does not completely get to grips with the question and lacks clarity and coherence of argument, and therefore would not gain either high-level AO2 or AO3 marks. The second paragraph is particularly confused. The discussion of the appointment process could be improved by some examples of appointments made (or rejected, such as Bork in 1987) for political reasons. Recent appointments to the court such as Sotomayor or Kagan would have been good examples to use. Some arguments need much more developed explanation as they are too vaguely asserted: for example, why would Alito's approval mean the court would be 'biased towards the conservatives'? What is a 'swing vote' on the court? Why are justices 'effectively making law' by their decisions? Who are the 'liberal' judges who 'won' in *Roe*? There is no discussion of judicial philosophies linking to politicisation arguments or the court's power of judicial review. The *Roe* case is a good choice but the student does not make the most of it. In fact, the third paragraph becomes largely unclear narrative, so the impact of the *Roe* v *Wade* decision in 1973 on the debate about politicisation is effectively lost. However, there is just enough **b** analysis and focus, with some backing evidence on the political role of justices in the USA, for the answer to achieve a low grade C.

Knowledge check answers

1 This important constitutional principle deriving from the work of Montesquieu is the idea that the three branches of government — executive, legislature and judiciary — should have separate functions, powers and personnel to avoid any concentrated power that would result in tyranny. This division of power between the branches, it is argued, leads to the need for greater compromise and consensus between the branches, or alternatively, potential gridlock in decision making.

2 Richard Neustadt argued that a complete separation of the executive and legislative powers in particular meant it would be impossible to operate a system of government decision making if the powers were exercised in totally independent branches. The US constitutional system implies an interdependent relationship between the two branches of government and a sharing of power, where decisions can only be made if the executive and legislative branches can work together.

3 Linked to the separation of powers and Madison's view that 'ambition will be used to counteract ambition', the power of one branch is used to check and balance the exercise of power by another, ensuring that no branch of government can dominate the federal government. Several checks and balances are in place to prevent the abuse of power, which the founders feared rather more than the inability to actually exercise it, which may be more of a problem in the USA today.

4 The constitution was deliberately designed to stand the test of time, imposing a slow, cumbersome and difficult formal amendment process that needed supermajorities in both houses of the federal legislature and also from the states. This was done in order to avoid ill-thought-out changes to the constitution in response to prevailing whims of the time. This it has managed to do, with only 17 formal amendments passed since the Bill of Rights in 1789.

5 The constitution contains several phrases that are vague and open to different interpretations at different times. The 8th Amendment's 'cruel and unusual punishment' has been interpreted differently regarding the application of the death penalty in different cases, pleasing some and displeasing others. Similarly, the 14th Amendment's 'equal protection of the laws' and 'due process' clauses have been at the heart of several controversial Supreme Court interpretations, including the *Brown* decision in 1954 and *Bush* v *Gore* in 2000.

6 The constitution has survived for over 220 years as an adaptive 'living' constitution, more flexible than is often stated. Apart from formal amendments passed through the amendment procedure, the vague words of the constitution are subject to Supreme Court interpretation that brings about constitutional change though 'interpretive amendments', and constitutional conventions have also evolved through usage. The short, vague document has provided the flexibility that the framers almost certainly desired, standing the test of time.

7 The constitution fragments power through the separation of powers, which fragments power between the branches of government, and also through the federal principle, which fragments power between the federal and state levels of government. This constitutional division of power into branches and layers of government creates a fragmented and divided power structure, in turn leading to numerous access points to government at both the federal and state levels.

8 The 16th amendment, ratified in 1913, allowed Congress the authority to levy a federal income tax, thus expanding the power of the federal government over the states, another factor leading to 'interdependence' rather than autonomy. The amendment vastly extended the spending power of the federal government because of growing demands for national services, and enhanced its fiscal power over state government, extending its economic role and responsibilities.

9 The 10th amendment relates to dual sovereignty and protects the power of the states to legislate under their 'reserved powers' in several areas, such as education and law and order, thus protecting their power within the federal system. It may be argued that these powers are less important today as the states are unable to deal with pressing economic problems needing federal intervention, such as air pollution, immigration and budgetary support. The 10th Amendment reflects tensions between central authority and local autonomy.

10 Liberals favour redistributive policies, including a more equal and fair distribution of resources from richer to poorer areas by a more powerful central government. They argue that economic inequalities in the USA need 'big' activist government power to reduce them and to regulate economic markets. Conservatives, who are more likely to be fiscal conservatives, believe that big government spending is wasteful, inefficient and insensitive to local needs, and that decisions need to be made closer to the people, with lower taxes and lower government spending.

11 The states remain important political units, preserving variety and distinctive political cultures, and running their own policy programmes in areas such as environmental protection, health care and penal policy. They can therefore be 'testing grounds' for new or untried policies, with liberal states like Massachusetts advancing a more liberal agenda, as seen in healthcare reform, and conservative states like Arizona a more conservative one, as seen in tougher immigration policies. They are testing new policies not yet ready for the national stage.

12 Signed into law by G. W. Bush in 2001 in the wake of the focus on national security after 9/11, the Patriot Act expanded the power and reach of US law enforcement agencies in counter-terrorism activities. It is criticised by civil liberties groups as unconstitutional, representing an unwarranted intrusion into civil rights and liberties guaranteed by the constitution. So far the Supreme Court has not made a judgement on the constitutionality of the Act.

13 Unlike most executive-dominated legislatures, such as the UK Parliament, the US Congress, because of the separation of powers, has independent powers granted to it by the constitution and holds the legislative power under Article 1.

This means that it is able to make policy through this legislative power rather than simply having some influence over the policies made by the separate executive branch. Even in changed conditions the Congress retains formidable independent power.

14 With their short 2-year terms of office, House members must continually please the voters in their districts to gain re-election through incumbency advantages rather than (or as well as) their party label. It is alleged this keeps them very close to their local electorates, who may closely follow their activities in DC, so they often act and vote with them in mind as 'all politics is local'. These are called 'home-style' activities.

15 Although the constitution gives Congress the legislative power, it is not practical for 535 individuals to initiate legislation that can satisfy national demands. Although most legislative proposals now originate from the executive branch, the separation of powers means they must be introduced in Congress by a sympathetic legislator on behalf of the president. However, he has little influence over what happens in Congress, which has the power to pass, reject or amend his legislative proposals.

16 The subcommittee stage is where bills can be significantly amended and pork-barrelled as the permanent members of the subcommittee, chosen for their expertise and constituency interests, attempt to add earmarks or 'riders' to the bill to benefit their constituents. This stage, involving detailed examination of the bill, usually sees influence from lobbyists representing special interests hoping to alter the bill in their favour through their evidence to the committee. The bill dies here if there is insufficient agreement to pass it.

17 The reconciliation procedure, done in an ad-hoc Conference Committee, is necessary to reconcile and compromise on the two different versions of a bill, passed concurrently, that have emerged from the very different chambers of the House and the Senate. This is because a single agreed bill, not two separate bills, must be sent to the president to be passed into law. The original Senate and House committees meet to reconcile their often very different bills, and if the bill cannot be reconciled then it dies.

18 Congress uses its constitutional powers to check the executive branch and hold it accountable for the implementation of policy. This oversight role is performed through control of taxation and spending, impeachment, and advice and consent powers, and through investigations by ad-hoc select committees such as those on 9/11 or the Iraq War as well as investigations done through its powerful standing committees. However, some argue that congressional oversight is limited by the complex nature of executive decision making and the vast resources of the executive branch.

19 Congress is organised into an elaborate committee structure where most of its work is carried out, but there is a hierarchy of committees and members compete for membership of the prestigious and powerful committees, as this can bring status to members and help with re-election. The most important committees are the financial ones deciding on taxation or spending and those with input into foreign policy or judicial appointment. House Rules is important as it determines the flow of legislation and has a 'gatekeeper' function.

20 Unlike British MPs, elected with a mandate from the party manifesto and financed by their party, members of Congress raise their own unlimited electoral finance and campaign largely on their personal views, despite standing under a party label. This means they do not have to 'toe a party line', are independent of party control in speaking and voting on issues, and cannot be forced to vote with their party.

21 The small amount of party leadership that exists through majority and minority leaders and whips has no effective sanctions or 'carrots and sticks' to use over the 435 independently elected and self-financing House members and 100 senators, who run personalised electoral campaigns and who are elected as Democrats or Republicans, but cannot be forced into voting the way the party wants them to.

22 The 'Contract with America', a conservative set of proposals that all Republican House candidates campaigned on in the 1994 mid-term election, led to more ideologically united congressional parties compared with their more bipartisan predecessors. Increasing partisanship and party control were seen in higher party unity scores on issues where a majority of one party opposed a majority of voters from the other party on roll-call votes. The Republican Party became a more cohesive conservative party and the Democratic Party a more liberal one.

23 Members of Congress have several competing pressures on them. Apart from the influence of the party under whose label they stood, members of Congress are exposed to other influences on their congressional voting, such as those from the voters in their districts and states who are the key to their re-election, from the interest groups who may have supported them financially at elections through their PACs, and from their own personal ideological views and consciences, when deciding what is the right political choice to make.

24 Home-style activities is the term for the constituency activities undertaken on behalf of the constituents who they represent in Congress, which dominate the activities of most members of Congress and take up much of their time and effort. It is these activities that members of Congress take credit for and emphasise to their electorates when they are up for re-election every 2 years. It is linked to pork barrelling, credit claiming and frequent trips back home to the district or state.

25 The resemblance model states that a representative assembly should be a social microcosm of the electorate that it has been elected to represent and should 'look like them' in socioeconomic and ethnic characteristics. In Congress there are very few young, female, ex-blue collar workers or black or Hispanic members compared to their percentage in the population as a whole, so Congress does not resemble the population in social terms.

26 While Congress has become more diverse in recent years, certain sections of US society are still significantly under-represented. These include women, Hispanics, younger and

low-income voters, and the non-religious. Congress is still a long way from looking like America.

27 The Founding Fathers wished to avoid a potentially tyrannical 'elected monarch' and too much power being exercised by one person. So they gave the president formal executive powers which were very vaguely framed (allowing for future development of the office) but at the same time ensured that these powers were checked and balanced by the independent power of Congress, so that there was no concentration of power and excessive power would be hard to wield.

28 Modern presidents have asserted their presidential power arising from the vague words in Article 2 during an economic or foreign policy crisis demanding clear leadership and quick, decisive action that cannot be provided by a 535-member, fragmented Congress which is highly attuned to constituency demands. It is usual in these circumstances for Congress to defer to the president, who takes the action thought to be necessary for the good of the nation, as happened during the great depression of the 1930s and after 9/11.

29 Presidents can only be removed from office by successful impeachment by Congress for proven 'high crimes and misdemeanors', where the House draws up the Articles of Impeachment and the Senate tries and convicts the president with a two-thirds majority. The president cannot be impeached or removed because of unsuccessful policies or political disagreements with Congress, unlike in the UK where a government can be removed by a successful vote of no confidence in parliament.

30 The Supreme Court's power of judicial review is a further check and balance on the exercise of presidential power and has been used several times when the court has accepted that the president has exceeded the power granted him by Article 2, ruling his actions 'unconstitutional' and therefore void. However, the court has not always used its power to check the president's actions, refusing to adjudicate in disputed areas such as the war powers.

31 Because of the two-term limit and fixed terms of office, presidents begin to lose power at the end of their first term as the need for re-election limits their freedom of action somewhat. More importantly, all presidents lose power at the end of their second term when there is no possibility of re-election, when approval ratings may be falling and especially when faced with a Congress dominated by the opposition party, as G. W. Bush was after the 2006 mid-terms produced a Democratic House and Senate.

32 This term distinguishes between the powers that a president is able to exercise in domestic policy compared with foreign policy. It is argued that all presidents try to 'tread the world stage' and are more likely to achieve successful outcomes when pursuing a foreign policy agenda, where Congress is more likely to defer to the 'commander-in-chief', than in domestic policy, where Congress is dominant and can more easily block the president's agenda.

33 A successful president, usually in his first year of office, would require a large electoral mandate, be a Washington insider, face a Congress dominated by his own party, and have high public approval ratings, excellent persuasion skills and favourable economic and foreign policy circumstances, or a crisis where the nation and Congress look to him for leadership.

34 Changing conditions led to the need for a vast administrative and political apparatus to support the president in fulfilling his executive role, including the expansion of the executive branch of government since government intervention in the economy in the 1930s and the growth of the USA into the 'world's policeman' since the 1940s. Institutions have developed such as EXOP and the huge federal bureaucracy in the expanded federal government departments and agencies that manage the modern state.

35 The constitution provides no executive role for the cabinet as it vests *all* executive power in the president and states that he 'may' seek their advice, with no constitutional requirement to do so. However, with the expansion of federal government departments since 1789 and the need for some coordination of policy between them, presidents have used their cabinets, albeit in a variable way, to cope with the pressures of modern decision making, although there is no collective decision making or responsibility as in the UK executive.

36 Most presidents are wary of the close links that develop between cabinet secretaries and their bureaucratic advisers and the congressional committees that oversee and fund them. This is known as 'agency capture'. As a result, most presidents turn to their more trusted and loyal advisers in EXOP who work only for the president, providing him with the more independent advice that he seeks and needs.

37 Most presidents express reservations about the unaccountable power of the federal bureaucracy and officials' entrenched views on policy, resulting from their specialist expertise built up over perhaps decades in a federal department or agency. They also distrust the close relationships between their cabinet secretaries and the permanent bureaucrats with whom they work closely.

38 These are justices who do not fit into the loose (liberal) or strict (conservative) constructionist categories and whose votes cannot be accurately predicted. They are crucial in the large number of cases decided by 5–4 majorities, where their vote tips the balance one way or another. Until 2005 the key swing justice was the more centrist Sandra Day O'Connor and since that time it has been Kennedy, both usually on the majority side of the 5–4 decisions and thus the crucial decisive vote.

39 Judicial independence makes the supreme court a valuable institution for settling constitutional conflicts that arise. Once on the court, the justices cannot be influenced or controlled by either of the two elected branches and cannot be removed for their judgements. Judicial independence is thus protected when making highly controversial decisions, which are bound to be greeted with opposition from one side or another of the political divide. Politicians may call for their impeachment, but they know that this cannot be done for reasons of their judicial decisions.

40 This judicially activist court made several politically controversial decisions, such as *Brown* and *Miranda*, based on loose construction, overturning precedent in many cases and bringing about significant social changes such as de-segregation. This was done not through legislative action by Congress but by the liberal decisions of the court forcing (eventually) social changes throughout the segregated south, provoking backlash and opposition from conservatives as well as galvanising the Civil Rights Movement.

41 This politically controversial case initiated the continuing debate between the 'pro-choice' and 'pro-life' lobbies. Abortion rights remain, despite being 'chipped away' at by subsequent court judgements, such as *Gonzales v Carhart* in 2007. *Roe* forms the basis of a woman's constitutional right to abortion, controversially found in the 'penumbras' of the constitution and implied 'privacy rights', and is criticised by strict constructionists as 'legislating from the bench'.

42 This highly politically charged case revolved around the manual recount of votes in Florida. The court decided that the recount of 'hanging chads' was unconstitutional, as it violated the 'equal protection' clause of the 14th Amendment, because there was not enough time to count all the disputed ballots. The five justices who voted to end the recount were all nominated by Republican presidents and the effect of their much-disputed judgement was that G. W. Bush became president, despite losing in the overall popular vote.

43 Be careful here. There is certainly evidence to suggest the Roberts' Court has been conservative in some areas, such as favouring corporate interests and the rights of gun owners, but it has also upheld the main provisions of Obamacare and has been positive on the issue of gay rights. It has also upheld the

1st Amendment rights of free speech and has failed to overturn *Roe v Wade*. Overall, its record to date has been mixed — 'consistently conservative' is certainly going too far as a verdict.

44 This 5–4 decision may be seen as an example of judicial activism because the court overturned two previous decisions regarding campaign finance, therefore overturning precedent as well as parts of the law passed by Congress and previously ruled constitutional. It is an example of the changing rightward direction of the court after the departure of Sandra Day O'Connor and the inclusion of the more judicially conservative Alito. It was criticised by President Obama as 'opening the floodgates to unlimited special interest money to influence the outcome of elections'.

45 A court's decision can only be overturned by a constitutional amendment gaining constitutionally required congressional and state supermajorities and so becoming part of the constitution that the Supreme Court must interpret, such as the 16th Amendment in 1913. However, the difficulty of reaching consensus on proposed constitutional amendments on issues such as abortion and flag burning makes this unlikely, although attempts are made, usually to express political disapproval of a court decision.

46 This is the term used when the court defers to the elected branches of government and refuses to consider politically controversial cases that it believes are best decided by the elected and accountable branches of government. There are many cases where the court has refused to grant certiorari (to be made more certain) and there is nothing to make the court agree to hear a case.

47 In *Bowers v Hardwick* in 1986, the court decided that Georgia's state law on homosexuality was constitutional. This decision was reversed in 2003 with the result that Georgia (and other states with similar laws) had to repeal their legislation.

Note: **bold** page numbers indicate definitions of key terms.